The
Readable Bible

Psalms

Liddell Press

Coming Soon

The Readable Bible: Pentateuch - *Winter 2013*

Visit ReadableBible.com to learn

about upcoming releases.

The Readable Bible

The Readable Bible is primarily a word-for-word translation of the Bible that renders the text as it would be spoken by a native English speaker and presents it in modern formats. Whenever a thought-for-thought translation is presented, the word-for-word translation is footnoted.

Psalms

Rodney S. Laughlin, editor

LIDDELL PRESS
Running for our Lord

Leawood Kansas

The Readable Bible Psalms

Copyright 2013 by Liddell Press. All rights reserved.

Published by: Liddell Press, www.liddellpress.com
                  12613 Pawnee Lane
                  Leawood, KS 66209
                  USA

ISBN: 978-1-939554-00-0 softcover edition

Library of Congress Control Number: 2012955897

Editor: Rodney S. Laughlin, rod-laughlin@liddellpress.com

Cover/Book Designer/Illustrator: Clyde Adams, www.clydeadams.com

Printed in USA

Contents

Preface

To The Reader

One day I was standing in an airport bookstore looking for a book to read. I asked myself, "Why am I looking for something to read when I have a Bible in my briefcase?" I answered, "The Bible is hard to read. I want to read something easier." Then I asked myself, "Why is it so hard to read? You're a seminary graduate, a pastor, a Bible teacher!" Thus began a quest that has led to The Readable Bible, the Bible as it would look if Moses, Joshua, Matthew, Mark, Paul and the other writers had been sitting in front of a PC when God spoke to them.

It seems to me that the Bible is hard to read because it presents all its material in sentence format. Today we use tables to present census information and charts for genealogies. When we want something built, we draw up a specification document. Law codes are organized in outline form. We use bullet points, bold text and other aids to help us grasp the information. Yet in today's Bibles all the information is still presented in sentence format in plain text. Surely those men of old would have used modern formats if they had been sitting in front of a PC when God spoke to them. Modern formatting does not change the information; it simply presents it in a way that makes it easier to grasp.

Translators have tried to make Scripture easier to read with new translation techniques. The New International Version uses a thought-for-thought method of translating in its effort to achieve functional equivalency. The New Living Translation moves further from the text, so far that many consider it a paraphrase. The Message, marketed as "a contemporary rendering of the Bible," is so far from the original words that a reader often has little idea of what the text actually says. While I lament the movement away from the actual words of the text, I celebrate how well these translations have been received.

But can't we make the Bible just as readable as these new Bibles without losing the actual text? I think we can, so I have set out to produce a Bible that is very readable, yet keeps the actual words of Scripture in front of the reader. However, there are times that a literal rendering of the text will be misunderstood by most readers. For instance, the vast majority of readers would not understand that when David wrote, "my kidney instructs me" (Ps. 16:7), he was referring to his innermost being. Today, if he were a native English speaker, he would say, "my heart instructs me." Thus, if we want our readers to understand the text, on occasion we must move from a literal translation to a thought-for-thought one. Whenever I have done this, I have footnoted the literal translation.

I have developed over one hundred principles of translation and presentation to produce an accurate yet very readable Bible. Some of these principles are discussed in the back of this book. I hope to discuss most of them in the Readable Bible Blog over the coming years. I am looking forward to our readers' comments and contributions. I am confident that some of you will have helpful suggestions that will be included in future editions.

My skills are not those of a professor. I am not a Hebrew or Greek scholar. But, by the grace of God, we have over four hundred English Bible translations today. In addition, there are many Hebrew and Greek language tools available in books and on the Internet. These have enabled me to look at every word and phrase in the original language and study the various ways scholars have rendered each one. The text you are about to read is the result of applying my translation, presentation and formatting principles to this information. Please take the time to read the short "Translation Principles" and "Format and Presentation Principles" articles at the back of the book. They are easy reading and will increase your understanding of the Biblical text.

You may struggle with the idea of Scripture in modern formats. I myself questioned whether it was proper to do this. After countless hours of investigating the history of Bible transcription and translation, I have become convinced that it is the natural and proper thing to do. So I have taken the plunge. With four years of work behind me and several in front of me to finish the project, I am hoping many of you will support this work by pre-ordering your copy of the complete Readable Bible at ReadableBible.com. I also hope you will visit the Readable Bible Blog and share your thoughts about how to make the Bible more readable.

My greatest hope in this project is that people who have never read the Bible will decide to read this one because it is so approachable. Please give a copy to someone who does not read the Bible.

Updates

Register your copy at ReadableBible.com. If you opt in, we will offer you the opportunity to purchase our future books of the Bible at a discount when they are released. We will also notify you whenever we post any changes, offer new editions or post explanatory material on our website or blog.

Dedication

I use the term "we" when writing about the production of The Readable Bible because many people are helping me produce it. Many dedicated Christians, some of whom I barely know, have spent hours editing, proofreading and making suggestions. I deeply appreciate their assistance. Yet no committee has produced this book. It is ultimately my work, and I accept full responsibility for all its weaknesses. I am sure that the work is not perfect, so I look forward to receiving constructive criticism from my readers.

And now I dedicate to Our Lord this attempt to translate his Holy Word, humbly asking him to grant that it may bring forth fruit to his glory and the building up of his people.

Rodney A. Laughlin

Editor
July, 2013

Introduction To Psalms[a]

Psalms is that unique book where we can all discover that we are just like the men of old. Like them,

Our hearts yearn to know God,

We grieve in our transgressions,

We ask for mercy when we go wrong,

We cry out for God's help when we are under pressure, and

We rejoice in The Lord when he delivers us.

Individuals, groups, and congregations have used psalms to express their hearts and minds to the Lord, and to each other. The one-hundred and fifty psalms gathered together in the Book of Psalms are the ones that Jewish believers accepted as inspired by God, and they all have been accepted as such by the Christian church. Some tell us about Israel's history and Israel's relationship with God. Some express complaints, calls for help, anguish, fear, faith, awe, joy and praise. Though all the psalms poured out of the hearts and minds of real people, each is the Word of God. Thus, each one gives us insight into our creator. In addition, every psalm gives us some insight into the inner and outer life of the psalmist. We see the reality, depth, strengths and weaknesses of his faith. We see his heart laid open in conversation with God.

Marvel at how the hearts of these men who lived thousands of years ago and live in Heaven today are no different than your own. As you read, join them by placing an open mind and heart before God.

Cascading Text

The Readable Bible formats each psalm as cascading text. This style will help you (a) find the meaning of the text, (b) see how phrases relate to each other, and (c) discover the rhythm of parallel phrases and thoughts.

Before You Read

Words in *italics* are additions to the text.

Please browse the Glossary before you begin reading. You will find lots of interesting information about words that appear in Psalms frequently, as well as important information regarding the words "Lord" and "YAHWEH."

We encourage you to read the "Principles of Translation" and "Format and Presentation Notes" in the back matter. They are easy reading and will increase your understanding of the text, especially the use of itallics..

---

a   "Psalms": a transliterated Greek word referring to songs accompanied by instruments. The Hebrew Bible title "Tehillim," means "Praises."

Psalms

BOOK ONE

Psalm 1
The Way of the Righteous

¹ Blessed is the man who does not
    Walk in the counsel of the wicked,
    Stand in the way of sinners, or
    Sit in a seat with scoffers.

² But
    His delight is in the law of the LORD, and
    On his law he meditates day and night.

³ He is like a tree planted by streams of water
    That yields its fruit in season, and
    Whose leaf does not wither.
  Whatever he does prospers.

⁴ The wicked are not so,
    But are like the chaff *a* that the wind drives away.

⁵ Therefore,
    The wicked will not stand in the judgment,
    Nor sinners in the assembly of the righteous.

⁶ For
    The LORD knows the way of the righteous,
    But the way of the wicked will perish.

Psalm 2
Warning to Kings and Judges

¹ Why do
    The *heathen* nations rage;
    The people plot in vain;
   ² The kings of the earth take their stand, and
    The rulers take counsel together
      Against the LORD and
      Against his anointed?
      They say,
       ³ "Let us break their chains and cast away their cords."

---

a "Chaff": the cover of the grain that is separated by threshing.

4 He who is enthroned** in the heavens laughs;
   The Lord scoffs at them.
5 In time he will
      Speak to them in his wrath;
      Terrify them with his fury;
      6 *And tell them,* "I have installed my king in Zion, upon my holy hill."

7 I will proclaim the Lord's decree, for he has said to me:
      "You are my Son;
      Today I have become your father.*^b*
      8 Ask me, and I will make
         The *heathen* nations your inheritance, and
         The ends of the earth your possession.
            9 You will break them with a rod of iron, shatter them like pottery."

10 Now therefore, you kings,
      Be wise.
   You rulers of the earth,
      Be warned;
      11 Serve the Lord with fear;
      Rejoice with trembling;
      12 Kiss the Son,*^c*
         So he will not be angry and you will not perish while on your way,
            For his wrath lights up quickly.

   Blessed are all who take refuge in him.

Psalm 3
Trusting God When in Trouble

A psalm of David.
Written when he fled from Absalom, his son.

   1 O Lord,
      How my foes have increased;
      So many rise up against me;
      2 So many say about my life,*^d* "God will not save him."   Selah
   3 But you, O Lord, are
      A shield around me,
      My glory, and
      The lifter of my head (*i.e., you hold up my chin*).

---

a   Literally, "who sits."
b   Literally, "I have begotten you."
c   "Kiss the son": a metaphor for giving homage to a king.
d   Or "of my soul."

⁴ I cried aloud to the LORD,
  And he answered me from his holy hill.   Selah
⁵ I lay down, sleep, and wake up;
  Because the LORD sustains me.
⁶ I will not be afraid *even if* ten thousand enemies surround me.*ᵃ*

⁷ Arise, O LORD;
 Save me, O my God;
  Strike all my enemies on the cheek;
  Break the teeth of the wicked.

⁸ Salvation comes from the LORD.
 May your blessing be upon your people.   Selah

Psalm 4
Standing for God

A psalm of David.
To the music director: *accompanied by* stringed instruments.

¹ O God of my righteousness,*ᵇ*
  Answer me when I call;
  Relieve me of distress;
  Have mercy on me, and
  Hear my prayer.

² O you children of men,
  How long will you
   Turn my glory into shame;
   Love what is worthless; and
   Chase after what is not true?   Selah
 ³ Know that
   The LORD has set apart the godly for himself;
   The LORD hears when I call to him.
 ⁴ Stand in awe, and do not sin;
   Commune with your own heart upon your bed, and be still; Selah
  ⁵ Offer righteous*ᶜ* sacrifices, and trust in the LORD.

⁶ Many say, "Who will show us any good?"
 But I say,

---

a Literally, "be afraid of ten thousand people set against me all around."

b Or "O righteous God."

c Or "right," or "proper."

"LORD,
>Lift up the light of your face[a] upon us.
>7 You have put gladness in my heart—more than *they have* when their grain and wine abound.
>8 I will lie down in peace and sleep,
>>For only you, O LORD, make me dwell in safety."

Psalm 5
A Cry for Help

A psalm of David.
To the music director: for flutes.

1 Listen to my words, O LORD;
Consider my groans.
2 Listen to my cry for help, my King and my God,
>For I am praying to you.
>>3 In the morning you hear my voice, O LORD;
>>In the morning I lay *my prayers*[b] before you;
>>And *then* I wait.
>4 For you are not a God who takes pleasure in wickedness.
>>Evil does not dwell in you;
>>>5 The arrogant do not stand before your eyes;
>>>You hate all who do evil;
>>>>6 You destroy those who tell lies;
>>>>You, the LORD, abhor men of blood and deceit.
7 As for me,
>I enter your house *only* because of your abundant lovingkindness;
>I bow down in fear toward your holy temple.

8 Guide me, O LORD, in your righteousness because of my enemies;
Make your way straight before me.
>9 For
>>There is no truth in their mouths;
>>Their inward *desires* are destructive;
>>Their throats are open graves; and
>>They flatter with their tongues.
10 Hold them guilty, O God;
Let them fall by their own counsels;
Cast them out because of the multitude of their transgressions,
>For they have rebelled against you.

---

a "Lift up the light of your face": an idiomatic expression meaning "smile."
b Or "my sacrifice."

¹¹ But let all those who take refuge in you rejoice;
Let them sing for joy forever;
Shelter^{*a*} them;
Let those who love your name rejoice in you.
 ¹² For you, O LORD, bless the godly;^{*b*}
 You surround them with your favor *like a* shield.

Psalm 6
A Sinner's Prayer of Distress

A psalm of David.
To the music director: on stringed instruments. According to sheminith.^{*c*}

¹ O LORD,
 Do not rebuke me in your anger, nor discipline me in your wrath.
  ² Have mercy upon me, O LORD, for I am slipping away.^{*d*}
LORD,
 Heal me, for my bones are in agony and ³ my soul is so troubled.
LORD,
 How long until you act?
⁴ LORD,
 Turn *to me;*
 Rescue my soul;
 Save me according to your lovingkindness,
  ⁵ For no one remembers you when they are dead.^{*e*}
   (Who gives praise to you from the grave?)
 ⁶ I am tired of my groaning.
  Every night my bed swims—I'm dissolving my couch in tears!
   ⁷ My eyes are blurred^{*f*} because of my grief, worn out because of all my enemies.

⁸ Get away from me, all you who do evil,
For
 The LORD has heard the sound of my weeping;
  ⁹ The LORD has heard my supplication;
 The LORD will receive my prayer.

¹⁰ All my enemies will be ashamed and deeply troubled.
They will turn back suddenly, in shame.

---

a   Literally, "cover."
b   Or "righteous."
c   "Sheminith": an undefined musical or liturgical term, or a tune or musical instrument.
d   Or "weak," or "weakening."
e   Literally, "there is no remembrance of you in death."
f   Literally, "waste away."

Psalm 7
Prayer of the Persecuted Victorious

A shiggaion[a] of David which he sang to the Lord regarding the words of Cush, the Benjaminite.

[1] O Lord my God,
  I take refuge in you;
  Save me from all those who persecute me;
  Deliver me,
    [2] So they do not
        Tear apart my soul like a lion and
        Drag me away[b] while there is no one to deliver me.

[3] O Lord my God, if I have done this:
  If there is injustice on my hands,
    [4] If I have rewarded a friend with evil,
  If I have plundered my enemy without cause;
  [5] *Then* let my enemy
        Pursue my soul and overtake it,
        Trample my life into the ground and
        Lay my glory in the dust.   Selah

[6] O Lord,
  Arise in anger;
  Rise up against the rage of my enemies;
  Wake up and command justice.
  [7] *Gather* the assembled peoples around you;
  Then return *to your throne* on high and *rule* over them.[c]

[8] The Lord judges people.[d]
  Judge me, O Lord,
  According to my righteousness, according to my integrity.
  [9] Oh righteous God who tests[e] hearts and minds,
    Let the wickedness of the wicked come to an end;
    Establish the just.[f]
[10] My shield is God *alone*, who saves the upright in heart.
[11] God is a righteous judge, a God who feels indignation every day.
[12] If the wicked[g] do not repent, God will sharpen his sword.
    He has bent his bow, *strung it* and made it ready.
    [13] He has prepared deadly weapons, *even* made flaming arrows.

---

a "Shiggaion": an undefined musical or liturgical term.
b Or "rip me to pieces."
c The Hebrew is not clear.
d Literally, "the peoples."
e Or "examines."
f Or "the righteous."
g Literally, "they."

¹⁴ Look,

> They conceive mischief, are pregnant with evil, and give birth to lies.
> ¹⁵ They *design* a pit *for others,* dig it, and fall into the hole they made.
> ¹⁶ Their mischief will backfire on their heads;
> Their violent *deeds* will come down upon their heads.

¹⁷ I will give thanks to the LORD because of his righteousness,
And I will sing praise to the name of the LORD most high.

Psalm 8

The Generosity of God

A psalm of David.
To the music director: *according to* gittith.*ᵃ*

¹ O LORD, our LORD,

> How majestic is your name throughout all the earth.
> You have set your glory above the heavens.
> ² Out of the mouth of babes and nursing infants you have ordained praise*ᵇ*
>> Because of your enemies,
>> To silence the enemy and the avenger.
> ³ When I consider
>> Your heavens,
>> The work of your fingers,
>> The moon and the stars which you set in place;
> ⁴ What is man, that you notice*ᶜ* him?
> And the son of man that you should take care of him?
> ⁵ For you have
>> Made him a little lower than the heavenly beings;*ᵈ*
>>> ⁶ Crowned him with glory and honor;
>>> Made him ruler over the works of your hands; and
>>> Put all things under his feet:
>>>> ⁷ All sheep and oxen, and also the beasts of the field;
>>>> ⁸ The birds of the air and the fish of the sea;
>>>> *And whatever* swims through*ᵉ* the ocean currents.*ᶠ*

⁹ O LORD, our LORD,

> How majestic is your name in all the earth.

---

a "Gittith": an undefined musical or liturgical term, or a tune or musical instrument.

b Literally, "you have established strength." We have used the Septuagint translation because it was quoted by Jesus (Mt. 21:16).

c Literally, "remember."

d Or "God."

e Literally, "passes through."

f Literally, "paths of the seas."

Psalm 9
A Joyful Song of Confidence in God

A psalm of David.
To the music director: *to the tune of* "Death of the Son."

¹ O LORD, I will
Give thanks to you with all my heart;
Tell of all your marvelous works;
² Be glad and rejoice in you; and
Sing praises to your name, O Most High.

³ My enemies turn back and fall and perish before your face;
⁴ For you have
Maintained my right and my cause;
Sat in the throne and judged righteously;
⁵ Rebuked the *heathen* nations;
Destroyed the wicked;
Blotted out their name forever and ever; and
⁶ Destroyed their cities so that the enemy has come to an end in everlasting
ruins—even the memory of them has perished.

⁷ The LORD reigns forever.
He has established his throne for justice;*a*
⁸ He will judge the world in righteousness; and
He will dispense *his judgments* to the people fairly.
⁹ The LORD is a refuge for the oppressed, a secure place in times of trouble.
¹⁰ Those who know your name trust in you, LORD;
For you do not forsake those who seek you.
¹¹ Sing praises to the LORD, who sits enthroned in Zion.
Proclaim his works among his people,
¹² For he who avenges murder*b* remembers them.
He does not forget the cry of the afflicted.

¹³ O LORD,
Have mercy*c* on me;
Look at my affliction—*see* their hate;
Lift me up from the gates of death,
¹⁴ That I may tell of it all—praising you in the gates of the daughter of
Zion—rejoicing in your salvation.

¹⁵ The *heathen* nations have fallen,
Fallen into the pit they dug and caught their foot in the net they hid!
¹⁶ The wicked are trapped by the work of their own hands!   Higgaion
The LORD is known for the judgments which he carries out.   Selah

---

a   Or "for judgment."
b   Literally, "blood."
c   Or "be gracious"

¹⁷ The wicked and all the nations that forget God will return to Sheol;
  ¹⁸ For the needy will not always be forgotten;
  The hope of the afflicted will not perish forever.

¹⁹ Arise, O Lord.
  Do not let man prevail;
  Let the *heathen* nations be judged before you.
    ²⁰ Put them in dread of you, O Lord,
      That the nations may know that they are but men.　　　　Selah

Psalm 10
Trusting God in the Midst of the Wicked

¹ O Lord,
  Why do you stand far away?
  Why do you hide yourself in times of trouble?
    ² The wicked arrogantly and fiercely chase after the poor.
  Let them be caught in the schemes they've devised.

³ The wicked person
  Boasts of his life's*^a* desire;
  Blesses the greedy and spurns the Lord; and
    ⁴ With a high nose, does not seek after *God.*
      All *his thoughts are,* "There is no god."
        ⁵ *He thinks* his ways are always prosperous;
          God's*^b* judgments are high above him, not in his sight.
        He sneers at his enemies.
      ⁶ He tells his heart, "I will never be moved, throughout all generations never
        have trouble."*^c*
      ⁷ His mouth is full of curses, deceit and oppression;
        Mischief and iniquity *hide* under his tongue.

      ⁸ He sits lurking in the villages, hiding, killing the innocent—his eyes
        watching for the unfortunate.
      ⁹ He lurks in hiding like a lion in its den to catch the afflicted.
          He draws them*^d* into his net and catches them;
            ¹⁰ They fall, sink down and are crushed by his might.*^e*
    ¹¹ He says in his heart,
      "God has forgotten.
      He is hiding his face;
      He will never see it."

---

a   Or "heart's," or "soul's."
b   Literally, "your."
c   Or "never be in adversity."
d   Literally, "the afflicted."
e   The Hebrew is not clear.

¹² O LORD,
>   Rise up;
> O God,
>>   Lift up your hand;
>>   Do not forget the afflicted.

>   ¹³ Why do the wicked spurn God and say in their heart, "He won't call me to account"?
>   ¹⁴ You have seen *the afflicted's* trouble and grief;
>>   You note it and take it in hand.
>>   The unfortunate commit themselves to you, you who help the fatherless.
>   ¹⁵ Break the arm of wicked and evil men;
>>   Call them to account for their wickedness until none are left.[a]

¹⁶ The LORD is king forever and ever;
> The *heathen* nations will vanish[b] from his land.
¹⁷ O LORD, you
>   Hear the desires of the humble;[c]
>   Turn your ear *to them* and strengthen their hearts;
>   ¹⁸ Dispense justice to the fatherless and the oppressed,
>>   So men who are of the earth may no longer terrify them.

Psalm 11
Trusting, Not Fleeing

A psalm of David.
To the music director.

>   ¹ I take refuge in the LORD;
>   So how can you say to me,[d] "Flee like a bird to the mountains?"
>   ² Look, the wicked
>>   Are stringing[e] their bows,
>>   Are fitting arrows to the string, and
>>   *Plan* to shoot the upright in heart when it's dark.
>   ³ If the foundations *of justice* are destroyed, what can the righteous do?

>   ⁴ The LORD is in his holy temple;
>   The LORD is on his throne in heaven.
>   His eyes see and his eyelids examine the children of men.
>   ⁵ The LORD tests[f] the righteous,

---

a   Literally, "you find none."
b   Literally, "will perish from."
c   Or "the afflicted."
d   Literally, "to my soul."
e   Literally, "bending."
f   Or "examines."

But

His soul hates the wicked, those who love violence.
6 He will rain fire and brimstone and snares upon the wicked;
A burning wind will be their portion.
7 For the LORD is righteous;
He loves justice;
And the upright will see his face.

Psalm 12
Prayer in the Midst of Vile Behavior

A psalm of David.
To the music director: to Sheminith.*a*

1 Help, LORD,
For the godly are disappearing;*b*
For the faithful are disappearing from among the children of men.
2 Everyone*c* lies to his neighbor, speaking with flattering lips and a double heart.

3 May the LORD cut off
All flattering lips and
Tongues that boast,*d* 4 saying:
"We will prevail with our tongues."
"Our lips are our own."
"Who is lord over us?"
5 "Now I will arise," says the LORD, "because of the devastation of the afflicted and the groaning of the needy.
I will set them in the safe place for which they long."

6 The words of the LORD are pure words;
Like silver refined*e* in a furnace, purified seven times.
7 O LORD, *we know that*
You will keep the godly,*f*
You will preserve them from this *lying* generation and forever
8 *Even though* the wicked strut about,
Even though disgusting behavior*g* is praised among the children of men.

---

a "Sheminith": an undefined musical or liturgical term, or a tune or musical instrument.
b Literally, "cease."
c Literally, "a man."
d Literally, "speaks of big."
e Literally, "tried."
f Literally, "them."
g Literally, "vileness."

Psalm 13
Singing When God Cannot Be Found

A psalm of David.
To the music director.

¹ O LORD
>How long will you forget me? Forever?
>How long will you hide your face from me?
>>² How long must I take counsel in my soul?^{*a*}
>>Every day I have sorrow in my heart—how long will my enemy gloat^{*b*} over me?
³ O LORD my God,
>Consider *my words* and answer me;
>Light up my eyes
>>Or I will sleep the sleep of death;
>>⁴ Or my enemy will claim, "I have overcome him";
>>Or my foes will rejoice when I am shaken.
>>⁵ For I have trusted in your lovingkindness; and
>>My heart rejoices in your deliverance.^{*c*}

⁶ I will sing to the LORD,
>Because he has treated me generously.

Psalm 14
The Fool

A psalm of David.
To the music director.

¹ The fool says in his heart, "There is no God."
>Such people^{*d*} are corrupt;
>They do abominable deeds;
>Not one does good.

² The LORD looks down from heaven at the children of men to see if there is anyone who understands, who seeks God.
³ But everyone has turned aside;
>Together they have become corrupt;
>There is no one who does good—not even one!

---

a "Counsel in my soul": an expression for mulling over one's own thoughts.
b Literally, "exalt."
c Or "rejoices in your salvation," or "rejoices that you have rescued me."
d Literally, "they."

4 Don't all the workers of iniquity have *any* knowledge,
> Those who eat up my people just as they eat bread?
> Those who have not called upon God?

Future Judgment of the Wicked

5 There the wicked*ᵃ* are in great fear,
> For God is with the righteous ones.*ᵇ*
6 You laughed at*ᶜ* the plan of the afflicted;*ᵈ*
> But the LORD *truly* is their refuge.

---

7 Oh that the salvation of Israel would come out of Zion now,
When the LORD restores his captive people, Jacob will rejoice; Israel will be glad.

Psalm 15
Who Abides With God?

A psalm of David.

1 Lord,
> Who will abide in your tent?
> Who will dwell on your holy hill?
>> 2 He who
>>> Walks blamelessly;
>>> Does what is right;
>>> Speaks the truth from his heart;
>>> 3 Does not slander with his tongue;
>>> Does not wrong his neighbor;
>>> Does not take up a reproach against his neighbor;
>>> 4 In his eyes despises a vile person;
>>> Honors those who fear the LORD;
>>> Swears an oath and does not change it when *keeping* it hurts;
>>> 5 Lends his money and does not charge interest;
>>> Does not take a bribe or besiege*ᵉ* the innocent.

> Whoever behaves this way*ᶠ* will never be shaken.

---

a   Literally, "they."
b   Literally, "the generation of the righteous."
c   Literally, "put to shame."
d   Or "of the poor."
e   Or "take a bribe against."
f   Literally, "whoever does these."

Psalm 16
Confidence in God Our Refuge

A miktam of David.

¹ Keep watch over me, O God,
For I take refuge *only* in you.
² I say to the LORD:
"You are my Lord; I have nothing good apart from you.
³ The godly ones in the land *of Israel,* those glorious people, they are all I
delight in.
(⁴ The sorrows of those who run after another god will increase.
I will not pour their drink offerings of blood;
I will not take their names upon my lips.)
⁵ LORD, you are my portion, my inheritance and my cup.
You determine*ᵃ* my lot *in life."*

⁶ The *boundary* lines have fallen in pleasant places for me;
Yes, I have a wonderful inheritance.*ᵇ*
⁷ I will bless the LORD who gives me counsel.
Even at night my heart*ᶜ* instructs me *about him.*
⁸ I have always set the LORD before me;
Because he is at my right hand, I will not be shaken.
⁹ Therefore
My heart is glad;
My whole being*ᵈ* rejoices and
My flesh rests in hope;
¹⁰ Because you will neither abandon my soul to Sheol nor allow your holy
one to see corruption.*ᵉ*
¹¹ You will show me the path of life;
In your presence there is fullness of joy;
At your right hand there are everlasting pleasures.

Psalm 17
Seeking Shelter in God

A prayer of David.

¹ O LORD,
Hear my just cause;
Listen to my cry;
Listen to my prayer—it is not from deceitful lips.

---

a   Or "support." Literally, "uphold."
b   Or "a beautiful heritage."
c   Literally, "kidney," which was seen as the seat of one's moral character, secret thoughts and feelings.
d   Literally, "my glory."
e   Or "see the pit."

2 May my vindication come from *what you see* before you;
May your eyes see what is right.

3 You have tried my heart;
You have visited me in the night;
You have tested me and found nothing *wrong.*
I am determined[a] that my mouth will not transgress.
4 As for the works of men,
By *following* your word[b] I've kept myself from the paths of the violent.
5 My steps have held to your paths, and my feet have not slipped.

6 O God,
I call upon you, for you will answer me.
Turn your ear, hear my words.
7 You who by your right hand saves those who take refuge in you from those who rise up against them,
Show me your wonderful lovingkindness;
8 Keep me as the apple of the eye;
Hide me in the shadow of your wings
9 From the wicked who destroy me;
From my mortal enemies who surround me;
10 For they
Are without feeling;[c]
Speak arrogantly;
11 Have now surrounded our steps; and
Look[d] to throw us to the ground 12 like a lion hungry for prey,[e] a young lion lurking in secret.

13 O Lord,
Arise;
Confront them;
Bring them down;
Deliver my soul
From the wicked by your sword;
14 From these men by your hand, O Lord;
From these men of the world whose portion is in this life.
You fill their wombs with treasure;
They are satisfied with children;
And they leave their abundance to their infants!

15 As for me,
In righteousness, I will behold your face;
When I awake, I will be satisfied with *seeing* your likeness.

---

a   Literally, "have purposed."
b   Literally, "the word of your lips."
c   Literally, "are closed."
d   Literally, "set their eyes."
e   Literally, "to tear."

Psalm 18
David's Song of Victory

To the music director.
A psalm of David, the servant of the Lord who addressed the words of this song to
the Lord on the day that the Lord delivered him from the hands of all his enemies,
even from the hand of Saul. He said:

¹ I love you, Lord, my strength.

² The Lord is
>> My rock,
>> My fortress,
>> My deliverer,
>> My God,
>> My rock in whom I take refuge,
>> My shield,
>> The horn of my salvation, and
>> My safe place.ᵃ
³ I call upon the Lord who is worthy of praise.
I am saved from my enemies.

⁴ Cords of death surrounded me;
Floods of destructionᵇ terrified me;
⁵ Cords of Sheol coiled around me;
Snares of death confronted me.
⁶ In my distress I called upon the Lord, cried out to my God;
He heard my voice from his temple;
My cry came before him, to his ears.

Then
⁷ The earth quaked and heaved;
The mountains' foundations shook and trembled;
>> Because he was angry *with my enemies.*
⁸ Smoke poured outᶜ of his nostrils, devouring fire from his mouth—coals lit up *all
around!*
⁹ He parted the heavens and came down—darkness under his feet—¹⁰riding a
mighty angel—flying—flying upon the wings of the wind!
¹¹ He made darkness his covering, his canopy around him—like thick clouds in the
skies!
¹² Brightness was *shining* in front of him; thick clouds passed *behind him—raining*
hailstones and coals of fire!
¹³ The Lord thundered from the heavens;
The Most High called out with his voice—hailstones and coals of fire!

---

a Or "stronghold."
b Or "ungodliness."
c Literally, "went out."

¹⁴ He shot his arrows and scattered them, and flashed lightning to rout his enemies.^{*a*}

¹⁵ At your rebuke, O LORD,
By the blast of breath from your nostrils,
 The valleys of the seas were laid bare;^{*b*} and
 The foundations of the world were exposed.

¹⁶ He
 Reached down^{*c*} from on high;
 Took me;
 Drew me out of deep^{*d*} waters and
 ¹⁷ Delivered me from powerful enemies who hated me, who were too strong for me.
  ¹⁸ They confronted me in the day of my calamity,
  But the LORD was my support.

¹⁹ He also brought me to a safe place.^{*e*}
He delivered me because he delighted in me.

²⁰ The LORD dealt with me according to my righteousness;
He rewarded me according to *my innocence,* the cleanness of my hands.

²¹ For
 I have kept the ways of the LORD;
 I have not acted wickedly before my God.
 ²² I *kept* all his judgments before me;
 I did not turn away from his statutes.
 ²³ I was upright before him;
 I kept myself from my iniquity.

²⁴ The LORD has rewarded me
 According to my righteousness,
 According to the cleanness of my hands before him.

²⁵ LORD,
 You show yourself
  Merciful to the merciful,
  Blameless to blameless,
  ²⁶ Pure to the pure, and
  Against^{*f*} the wicked.
 ²⁷ For you will save the humble,
 But will bring down the proud.^{*g*}

---

a Literally, "them."
b Literally, "were seen."
c Literally, "sent."
d Literally, "many."
e Literally, "brought me out into a spacious place."
f Literally, "perverse to."
g Literally, "bring down those with haughty eyes."

²⁸ You light my lamp;
You, the LORD my God, light up my darkness.
²⁹ With you I can run through a band *of the wicked,* and
By you, my God, I can *even* leap over a wall!

³⁰ As for God,
His way is perfect;
For the word of the LORD has proven true.
He is a shield to all those who take refuge in him,
³¹ For who is God except the LORD?
And who is a rock except our God?
³² He is the God who
Arms*ᵃ* me with strength,
Makes my way perfect,
³³ Makes my feet like the feet of a deer,
Stands me up in high places ³⁴ and
Trains my hands for battle—my arms can *even* bend a bronze bow!

³⁵ You have given me the shield of your salvation;
Your right hand has held me up;
Your gentleness has made me great;
³⁶ You lengthened my stride*ᵇ* and my feet did not slip.
³⁷ I pursued my enemies and overtook them;
I did not turn back until they were destroyed.
³⁸ I shattered them so that they were not able to rise, and
They fell under my feet.
³⁹ You have equipped me with strength for battle;
You have subdued under *my feet* those who rose up against me;
³⁹ You have made my enemies turn their backs, that I might
Destroy those who hate me;
(⁴¹ They cried, but there was no one to save them.
They cried, even to the LORD, but he did not answer them.)
⁴² Beat them as fine as the dust in the wind; and
Cast them out as the dirt in the streets.
⁴³ You have delivered me from strife with the people, and
You have made me the head of the *heathen* nations.
A people I did not know serve me.
⁴⁴ As soon as they hear me, they obey me.
Foreigners cower in fear before me—⁴⁵they*ᶜ* lose heart and come out
of their fortresses trembling!

⁴⁶ The LORD lives;
Blessed be my Rock;
Exalted be the God of my salvation.

---

a   Literally, "girds."
b   Literally, "widen my step under me."
c   Literally, "the foreigners."

⁴⁷ For God

>Avenges me,
>Subdues peoples under me,

⁴⁸ Delivers me from my enemies,

>Yes, lifts me up above those who rise up against me; and
>Rescues me from violent men.

⁴⁹ Therefore I will praise you, O LORD, among the nations,

>And sing praises to your name, *singing out,*

>>⁵⁰ "He gives his king great victories.

>>He shows lovingkindness to his anointed, to David and his descendants forever."

Psalm 19
The Heavens Declare

A psalm of David.
To the music director.

¹ The heavens declare the glory of God, and
The skies declare the work of his hands.

>² Day after day they pour out their words;
>Night after night they declare their knowledge.

>>³ There is no speech nor language*ᵈ* in which their voice is not heard.

>>⁴ Their message*ᵇ* has gone throughout the earth, and
>>Their words *reach* the ends of the world.

In the heavens*ᶜ* he has pitched a tent for the sun, which

>⁵ Comes out of his chamber like a bridegroom rejoicing, like an athlete*ᵈ* running a race;

>⁶ Rises at one end of the heavens and follows its course*ᵉ* to the other end, *leaving* nothing hidden from its heat.

His law Is Perfect.

⁷ The law of the LORD is perfect,

>Reviving*ᶠ* the soul;

The testimony of the LORD is perfect,

>Making wise the simple;

⁸ The precepts of the LORD are right,

>Bringing joy to the heart;

---

a   Literally, "words."
b   Literally, "line"; or "cord."
c   Literally, "them."
d   Literally, "strong man."
e   Literally, "circuits."
f   Or "restoring."

The commands of the LORD are pure,
> Enlightening the eyes;
⁹ The fear of the LORD is pure,
> Enduring forever;
The judgments of the LORD are
> True and righteous altogether;
> ¹⁰ To be desired more than gold, yes, *more than* lots of pure gold;
> Sweeter than honey dripping off the honeycomb.
¹¹ Your servant is warned by them, and
There is great reward in keeping them.
¹² Who can understand his own errors *without them?*

Declare me innocent, cleansed*ᵃ* of my hidden *faults*;
¹³ Hold back your servant from presumptuous*ᵇ sins*.
> Don't let them rule over me;
> Then will I be blameless, innocent of great transgression.

¹⁴ O LORD, my strength and my redeemer, let the words of my mouth and the meditation of my heart be acceptable in your sight.

Psalm 20
Prayer for the King

A psalm of David.
To the music director.

¹ May the LORD answer you in times of trouble;
May the name of the God of Jacob
> Protect you;
> ² Send you help from his sanctuary;
> Give you support from Zion;
> ³ Remember all your offerings and accept your burnt sacrifices;   Selah
> ⁴ Grant *good things* to you according to *the desires of* your heart; and
> Fulfill all your plans.
Then
> ⁵ We will shout*ᶜ* for joy over your victory, and
> We will raise up our banners in the name of our God.
May the LORD fulfill all your requests.

⁶ Now I know that the LORD saves his anointed;
> He will answer him from his holy heaven with the saving strength of his right hand.
⁷ Some trust in chariots, some *trust* in horses,
> But we trust in the name of the LORD our God.

---

a   The Hebrew word "naqah" contains both meanings, "cleanse" and "declare innocent."
b   "Presumptuous": done with boldness and total disregard of what is right.
c   Or "sing."

⁸ They are brought down and fall,
    But we rise up and stand upright.

⁹ O Lᴏʀᴅ, save the king.
    May the Lᴏʀᴅ*ᵃ* answer us when we call.

Psalm 21
Thanksgiving for the King's Success

A psalm of David.
To the music director.

¹ O Lᴏʀᴅ
    The king rejoices in your strength;
    How greatly I rejoice in your victories.
  ² You have
        Given me my heart's desire, not withheld my lips' request;   Selah
      ³ Welcomed me with rich blessings; and
        Set a crown of pure gold on my head.
  ⁴ I asked you for life, and you gave it to me—length of days forever and ever.
  ⁵ My glory is great because of your victories.
    Splendor and majesty have been bestowed upon me; ⁶ for
        You have granted me eternal blessings;*ᵇ* and
        You have made me glad with the joy of your presence.
  ⁷ The king trusts in the Lᴏʀᴅ;
    I will not be moved
        Because of the lovingkindness of the most high.

⁸ Your hand will seize*ᶜ* all your enemies;
  Your right hand will seize those who hate you;
⁹ You will make them *burn* as *if in* a fiery furnace at the time of your appearing;
  You, Lᴏʀᴅ, will swallow them up in your wrath.
        Fire will devour them, ¹⁰ wipe*ᵈ* their descendants from the earth, from
        mankind;*ᵉ*
      ¹¹ Because they plotted evil against you, devised a wicked scheme that will not
        succeed.
¹² You will make them turn their backs *and run* when you aim your bows at their
  faces.

¹³ Be exalted, O Lᴏʀᴅ in all your might;
  We will sing and praise your power.

---

a   Literally, "he."
b   Or "have made him most blessed."
c   Literally, "find out." Picture a hand reaching into a void to grab something hidden from sight. And
    next line.
d   Literally, "destroy."
e   Literally, "from the children of men."

Psalm 22
The Suffering Servant

A psalm of David.
To the music director: *to the tune of* "Deer of the Dawn."

¹ My God, my God,
  Why have you forsaken me?
  Why are you so far from saving me, *so far* from the words of my groaning?
² O my God,
  I cry out in the daytime, but you do not answer;
  And in the nighttime, but find no rest.[a]

³ You, you who are enthroned on the praises of Israel, are holy.
  ⁴ Our fathers trusted in you.
    They trusted, and you delivered them;
    ⁵ They cried to you, and were delivered;
    They trusted in you, and were not put to shame.
⁶ But I am
  A worm, not a man;
  Scorned by men, despised by the people.
  ⁷ All who see me mock and sneer[b] and wag their heads, *saying:*
    ⁸ "He trusts in the Lord to deliver him.
      Let God[c] deliver him, for he delights in the Lord."[d]
⁹ Yet
  You are the one[e] who brought me out of the womb;
  You made me trust you while at my mother's breasts.
    ¹⁰ I was cast upon you at my birth;[f]
  You have been my God from my mother's womb.
¹¹ Do not be far from me,
  For trouble is near and there is no one to help;
  ¹² Many bulls surround me;
    Strong bulls of Bashan encircle me;
    ¹³ Like ravening lions, they open their mouths wide—roaring.
  ¹⁴ I am poured out like water;
  All my bones are out of joint;
  My heart is like wax;
  My insides are melting;[g]
  ¹⁵ My strength is dried up like sunbaked clay;[h]

a Or "and am not silent."
b Literally, "separate their lips."
c Literally, "him."
d Literally, "delights in him."
e Literally, "he."
f Literally, "from the womb."
g Literally, "melting within my bowels."
h Literally, "like a potsherd." "Potsherd": a piece of broken pottery.

My tongue sticks to my jaws;
You have laid me in the dust of death.
¹⁶ *Wild* dogs*ᵃ* have surrounded me;
A band of wicked men have encircled me;
They have pierced my hands and my feet;
¹⁷ I can count all my bones;
They look, staring at me;
¹⁸ They divide my garments among themselves; and
They cast lots for my clothes.
¹⁹ O Lᴏʀᴅ,
Do not be far away;
O My Strength,
Come quickly to help me;
²⁰ Deliver my soul from the sword, my precious*ᵇ* life from the power of these dogs;
²¹ Save me from this lion's mouth, from the horns of this wild ox.

²² I will proclaim your name to my brothers;
I will praise you in the midst of the congregation *like this*:

²³ "You who fear the Lᴏʀᴅ, praise him;
All you descendants of Jacob, glorify him;
All you the descendants of Israel, fear him.
²⁴ For
He has neither regarded with contempt nor been repulsed by the suffering of the afflicted;
He has not hidden his face from them;
He has heard the afflicted*ᶜ* when they cried for help."

²⁵ My praise in the great assembly will be of you;
I will fulfill my vows before those who fear you.
²⁶ The lowly will eat and be satisfied;
Those who seek the Lᴏʀᴅ will praise him—may their hearts live forever.
²⁷ All the ends of the earth will remember the Lᴏʀᴅ and turn to him;
All the families of the nations will bow down before him;
²⁸ For kingship*ᵈ* is the Lᴏʀᴅ's *only*—he rules over the nations.
²⁹ The rich on the earth will eat and worship;
All those whose lives end up as dust*ᵉ* will bow before him;
For no one can keep himself*ᶠ* alive *forever*.

---

a   Dogs were not domesticated in Israel at this time.
b   Literally, "only."
c   Literally, "them."
d   Or "royal power."
e   Literally, "who go down to the dust."
f   Literally, "his soul."

[30] *Our* descendants
  Will serve the Lord,
  Will tell *future* generations about him, and
[31] Will come and will declare his righteousness and *the things* that he has done.

Psalm 23
The Shepherd's Psalm

A psalm of David.

[1] The LORD is my shepherd;
  I shall not want.
  [2] He makes me lie down in green pastures;
  He leads me beside still waters;
  [3] He restores my soul;
  He leads me in the paths of righteousness for his name's sake.
[4] Even though I walk through the valley of the shadow of death,
  I will fear no evil;
  For
    You are with me;
    Your rod and your staff, they comfort me;
    [5] You prepare a table before me in the presence of my enemies;
    You anoint my head with oil—my cup overflows.
[6] Surely goodness and lovingkindness[a] will pursue[b] me all the days of my life,
  And I will dwell in the house of the LORD forever.

Psalm 24
He Is the King of Glory

A psalm of David.

[1] The earth is the LORD's, and all it contains;
  The world *is the LORD's,* and those who live on it;
[2] For he founded it upon the seas
  And established it upon the rivers.

[3] Who will ascend the mount of the LORD?
  Who will stand in his holy place?
  [4] He who has clean hands and a pure heart;
  He who does not lift up his soul to vanity or swear deceitfully;
  [5] He will receive blessing from the LORD, righteousness from the God of his
    salvation.
    [6] Such is the generation of those who seek him, who seek your face, O *God
    of* Jacob.   Selah

---

a   Or "mercy."
b   Or "follow."

⁷ Lift up your heads, O you gates;
　　Be lifted up, you ancient doors,
That the King of glory may come in.
　　　Who is this King of glory?
　　　　　The LORD—strong and mighty.
　　　　　The LORD—mighty in battle.
　⁹ Lift up your heads, O you gates;
　　Lift them up, you ancient doors,
　　　　That the King of glory may come in.
　¹⁰ Who is this King of glory?
　　　The LORD of hosts;
　　　　He is the King of glory.

8

Selah

Psalm 25
A Prayer for Pardon

A psalm of David.

　¹ To you, O LORD, I lift up my soul;
　² O my God, I trust in you.
　　　Do not let me be put to shame;
　　　Do not let my enemies triumph over me.
　　　　³ Indeed, no one who waits on you will be put to shame,
　　　　　But those who act treacherously without cause will be ashamed.
　　O LORD,
　　　⁴ Show me your ways;
　　　Teach me your paths;
　　　⁵ Guide me in your truth; and
　　　Teach me;
　　　　　Because you are the God of my salvation;
　　　　　And I wait all day long for you.
　⁶ Remember, O LORD, your compassion and your lovingkindness,
　　　For they are from old.
　⁷ Do not remember the sins of my youth, my transgressions;
　　Remember me according to your lovingkindness
　　　For the sake of your goodness, O LORD.

　⁸ The LORD is good and upright.
　　Therefore he
　　　Teaches sinners about his ways;^a and
　　　⁹ Guides the lowly in justice, teaching them^b his way.

---

a　Or "in the way."
b　Literally, "teaches the lowly."

¹⁰ All the ways of the LORD are *out of his* lovingkindness and faithfulness*ᵃ* toward*ᵇ*
those who keep his covenant and *agree with* what he says.*ᶜ*
¹¹ O LORD, for your name's sake, pardon my iniquity, for it is great.

¹² Who is the man that fears the LORD?
God will instruct him about the path*ᵈ* that he should choose;
¹³ His soul will dwell in goodness;
And his descendants will inherit the land.
¹⁴ The counsel*ᵉ* of the LORD is with those who fear him,
And he makes his covenant known to them.

¹⁵ My eyes are always *looking* toward the LORD,
For he will free my feet from the traps *of my enemies.*

¹⁶ Turn to me and have mercy,
For I am lonely and afflicted;
¹⁷ The troubles of my heart are increasing.
Bring me out of my distresses;
¹⁸ Look upon my affliction and my trouble; and
Forgive all my sins.

¹⁹ Consider my enemies,
For there are many; and
They hate me violently.
²⁰ Guard my soul and deliver me;
Do not let me be put to shame,
For I take refuge in you.
²¹ Let integrity and uprightness protect me,
For I wait on you.

²² O God, redeem Israel out of all its troubles.

Psalm 26
A Call for Vindication

A *psalm* of David.

¹ Vindicate me, O LORD,
For I have walked in personal integrity;*ᶠ*
I have trusted in the LORD without wavering.
² Examine me, O LORD;
Test me, try me;

---

a Or "truth."
b Or "to," or "for."
c Literally, "keep his covenant and his testimonies."
d Or "in the way."
e Or "friendship."
f Literally, "my integrity."

Burn pure my conscience[a] and my heart.
3 For

 Your lovingkindness is before my eyes; and
 I walk in your truth.[b]
   4 I do not sit with vain persons,
     Nor do I associate[c] with hypocrites.
   5 I hate the gatherings of those who do evil, and
     I do not associate[d] with the wicked.
  6 I wash my hands in innocence, and
  I walk[e] around your altar, O LORD,
    7 To proclaim *your glory* with a voice of thanksgiving;
      to tell of all your wondrous works.

8 O LORD,
 I love your house, the place where your glory dwells.
  9 Do not take away my soul with sinners, nor my life with bloodthirsty men
   10 Whose hands *hold* wickedness,
     Whose right hands are full of bribes.
      (11 But as for me, I walk in personal[f] integrity.)
  Redeem me and be gracious to me.

12 My foot stands on level ground.
 In the congregation[g] I will bless the LORD.

Psalm 27
The Lord is My Light and My Salvation

A *psalm* of David.

 1 The LORD is my light and my salvation, whom shall I fear?
 The LORD is the stronghold of my life, of whom shall I be afraid?
   2 When evildoers come to devour my flesh, they (my adversaries, my foes) will
     stumble and fall.
   3 Though an army sets up camp against me, my heart will not fear.
     Though war should rise against me, I will be confident.

 4 One thing I ask of the LORD;
 One thing I seek:
     That I may dwell in the house of the LORD all the days of my life

---

a Literally, "my kidney," the part of the body which they envisioned as the repository of one's moral
   character, of one's secret thoughts and feelings.
b Or "your faithfulness."
c Literally, "sit."
d Literally, "sit."
e Literally, "go."
f Literally, "walk in my."
g Or "great assembly."

To gaze upon the beauty of the LORD,
To inquire^a *of him* in his temple.
5 For in the day of trouble
He will hide me in his shelter;
He will hide me under his covering, his tent;
He will lift me up upon a rock.
6 Then
My head will be lifted up above my enemies all around me;
I will offer sacrifices before his tent with shouts of joy; and
I will sing, sing praises to the LORD.

7 O LORD,
Hear when I cry with my voice;
Be gracious to me; and
Answer me.

8 When you said, "Seek my face," my heart said, "LORD, I will seek your face."
9 Do not hide your face far from me;
Do not reject^b your servant in anger,
For you have *always* been my helper.
Do not leave me or abandon me, O God of my salvation.

10 Though my father and my mother forsake me, the LORD will receive me.

11 O LORD,
Teach me your way;
Lead me on a level path because my enemies *lie waiting for me*;
12 Do not abandon me to the desire of my enemies;
For false witnesses breathing violence have risen against me.

13 Unless I'd believed I'd see the goodness of the LORD in the land of the living ...^c

14 Wait on the LORD;
Be strong;
Be strong-hearted; and
Wait on the LORD.

Psalm 28
The Lord is My Strength

A psalm of David.

1 O LORD, my rock,
I am crying out to you;

---

a Or "to seek him."

b Literally, "stretch out against," meaning to turn someone away.

c Literally, "unless I had believed." The text leaves the sentence unfinished, perhaps so the reader can fill in his thought. Most translations either add a thought such as "I would have fainted" or "despaired," or convert the verse into a statement of confidence in seeing "the Lord in the land of the living."

Do not be deaf to me.
> If you are silent, I will become like those who go down into the pit.
2 Hear the voice of my appeals[a]
> When I cry to you,
> When I lift up my hands toward your holy sanctuary.[b]
3 Do not drag me away with the wicked, with the workers of iniquity
> Who speak peace to their neighbors when evil is in their hearts.
4 Repay them according to their deeds, *according to* the evil of their endeavors;
Repay them for the work of their hands;
Recompense them, returning like for like;
>> 5 Because they have no regard for your work, LORD, or the things you have made[c]

Tear them down and don't build them up *again.*

6 Blessed be the LORD,
> Because he has heard my cry for mercy.
7 The LORD is my strength and my shield;
My heart trusts him, and he helps me.[d]
My heart exults greatly, thanking him with songs.
8 The LORD is the strength of his people,[e] the saving refuge of his anointed.

9 LORD,
> Save your people;
> Bless your inheritance;
> Be their shepherd and carry them forever.

Psalm 29
Ascribe to the Lord

A psalm of David.

1 Ascribe[f] to the LORD, O you heavenly beings,
> Ascribe to the LORD glory and strength;
> 2 Ascribe to the LORD the glory due his name;
Worship the LORD in the splendor of his holiness.

3 The voice of the LORD
> Is over the waters.
>> The God of glory thunders;
>> The LORD is over many waters.

---

a   Literally, "my supplications."
b   Or "Most Holy Place," the innermost room of the temple, where God dwelt.
c   Literally, "not the works of his hands."
d   Literally, "I am helped."
e   Literally, "is their strength."
f   "Ascribe": credit a person with having.

⁴ The voice of the Lord

    Is powerful;

    Is full of majesty and

    ⁵ Breaks the cedars.

        The Lord breaks the cedars of Lebanon into pieces;

          ⁶ He makes *the cedars of* Lebanon *appear to* leap like a calf;*^a*

        Even Mount Hermon*^b seems to leap* like a young wild ox.

⁷ The voice of the Lord

    Strikes*^c* with flames of fire and

    ⁸ Shakes the wilderness.

        The Lord shakes the wilderness of Kadesh.

⁹ The voice of the Lord

    Terrifies the deer*^d* and

    Strips the forest bare.

  In his temple every one cries, "Glory!"

¹⁰ The Lord sits enthroned over the floodwaters;

  The Lord sits enthroned as King forever.

¹¹ The Lord gives strength to his people;

  The Lord blesses his people with peace.

Psalm 30
Thanksgiving for Restoration

A psalm of David.
A song for the dedication of the temple.

  ¹ Lord, I will exalt you,

      For you have lifted me up and have not allowed my foes to rejoice over me.

  ² Lord my God, I cried to you for help and you healed me.

  ³ Lord, you have brought my soul up from Sheol, kept me alive that I should not go down to the pit.

  ⁴ You saints,

     Sing praises to the Lord;

     Praise his holy name.

      ⁵ For His anger lasts *only* a moment, but his favor lasts for a lifetime;

       Weeping may last for a night, but joy comes with the morning.

  ⁶ When I was prospering I said, "I will never be shaken."

  ⁷ By your favor, Lord, you made my mountain stand firm;

  Then you hid your face, and I was dismayed.

---

a   This line and the next refer to God's power as the trees are tossed about, creating a scene that from a distance looks like animals leaping.

b   Literally, "Sirion," a name for Mt. Hermon.

c   Literally, "hews out flames."

d   The Hebrew word "chuwl" means to writhe in pain, and thus is often interpreted as, "to give birth." The emphasis here is on the awesome power of the LORD, so we render it as "terrifies."

⁸ *So*

I cried out to you, LORD;

I pleaded with you, LORD, *saying:*

⁹ "What do you profit from my life*ᵃ* when I go down to the pit?

Will the dust praise you or proclaim your truth? *ᵇ*

¹⁰ Hear me, LORD, and have mercy upon me;

O LORD, be my helper."

¹¹ Then

You turned my mourning into dancing;

You took off*ᶜ* my sackcloth and clothed*ᵈ* me with gladness

¹² Such that my soul sings praises to you and cannot be silent.

O LORD my God, I will give you thanks forever.

Psalm 31
Prayer of Trust in God

A psalm of David.
To the music director.

¹ LORD, I take refuge in you.

Let me never be put to shame;

Deliver me in your righteousness;

² Listen*ᵉ* to me;

Rescue me quickly;

Be my strong rock of refuge, a strong fortress to save me.

³ You are my rock and my fortress.

Therefore, for your name's sake,

Lead me;

Guide me;

⁴ Pull me out of the net they have secretly laid for me;

For you are my refuge.

⁵ Into your hands I commit my spirit.

For you have redeemed me,*ᶠ* O LORD, faithful God.

⁶ I hate those who pay regard to worthless idols;

I trust in the LORD.

⁷ I will be glad and rejoice in your lovingkindness,

For you

Have considered my affliction;

Have known the anguish of my soul;

---

a   Literally, "blood."

b   Or "your faithfulness."

c   Literally, "loosed."

d   Literally, "girded."

e   Literally, "incline your ear."

f   Or "redeem me."

⁸ Have set my feet in a safe place^{*a*}
  Rather than give^{*b*} me over to the hands of the enemy.

⁹ O Lord, have mercy upon me, for I am in distress.
  My eye, my body, my soul—they waste away from grief;
    ¹⁰ My life is spent in sorrow, my years in sighing;
  My strength fails because of my iniquity; and
  My bones waste away.
    ¹¹ I am
      A reproach among all my enemies, especially my neighbors;
      Dreaded by my acquaintances—they flee when they see me in the street!
        ¹² Forgotten, out of *everyone's* mind like a dead man or broken jar.
    ¹³ I hear the whispering of many (terror is all around me!) conspiring together
    against me, scheming to take my life.

¹⁴ But I trust in you, O Lord, declaring,
  "You are my God;
    ¹⁵ My future is^{*c*} in your hands."
  Deliver me from the hand of my enemies and those who persecute me;
¹⁶ Make your face shine on your servant;
In your unfailing love, save me.

¹⁷ O Lord,
    Do not let me be put to shame, for I have cried out to you;
    Let the wicked be put to shame, silenced until *they end up in* Sheol;
      ¹⁸ Let the lying lips that proudly speak against the righteous with contempt and
      arrogance be put to silence.

¹⁹ Oh how abundant is your goodness!
Your goodness,
    Which you have stored up for those who fear you;
    Which you use^{*d*} in the sight of everyone^{*e*} for those who take refuge in you;
      ²⁰ Hiding them from the plots of men under the cover of your presence,
      Keeping them in your shelter, *safe* from the strife of tongues.

²¹ Blessed be the Lord, for he showed his lovingkindness in a besieged city.
    ²² When I panicked and cried out, "I am cut off from your sight,"^{*f*}
    When I cried out he heard my voice, my pleas.
²³ Love the Lord, all you godly ones,
    For the Lord preserves the faithful and fully repays the proud.
²⁴ Be strong;
Take heart, all you who hope in the Lord.

---

a   Literally, "a spacious place."
b   Literally, "and have not given."
c   Literally, "my times are."
d   Literally, "you give."
e   Literally, "before the sons of men."
f   Literally, "from before your eyes."

Psalm 32
The Blessing of Forgiveness

A psalm of David. A maskil.

1 Blessed is he whose
  Transgression is forgiven,
  Whose sin is covered.
2 Blessed is the man
  Against whom the LORD counts no iniquity,
  In whose spirit is no guile.
3 When I kept silent,
  My bones wasted away while I groaned all day long.
    4 For day and night your hand was heavy upon me.
  My strength was dried up as if in the heat of summer.　Selah
5 Then
  I acknowledged my sin before you;
  I ceased hiding my iniquity;
  I said *to myself,* "I will confess my transgressions to the LORD."
And you forgave the iniquity of my sin.　Selah
6 Likewise, let everyone who is godly pray to you
  In this time when you can be found,
    For in the floods of great waters they will not *be able* to reach you.

7 You are my hiding place;
You will protect me from trouble;
You will surround me with songs of deliverance.　Selah

The Lord says,
  8 I will instruct you and teach you in the way you should go;
  I will counsel you with my eye *on you.*
  9 Do not be like a horse or a mule,
    Who has no understanding,
    Whose harness includes a bit and bridle to control him,
      Without which he is uncontrollable.[a]

10 Many are the sorrows of the wicked,
  But lovingkindness surrounds those who trust in the LORD.
11 All you righteous ones,
  Rejoice in the LORD and be glad;
All you who are upright in heart,
  Shout *praises* joyfully.

---

a　Literally, "he will come about."

Psalm 33
Rejoice in the Lord

¹ You righteous *ones,*
  Sing out in joy to the LORD,
    For praising *God* is appropriate for the upright;
  ² Give thanks to the LORD with harp;
  Sing to him with the ten-stringed lyre;
  ³ Sing a new song to him;
  Play skillfully and sing*ᵃ* with joy.
  ⁴ For
    The word of the LORD is right;
    All his works are fair.*ᵇ*
      ⁵ For he loves righteousness and justice.
    The earth is full of the lovingkindness of the LORD.
      ⁶ By the word of the LORD the heavens were made,
        And all their multitude of stars by the breath of his mouth;
      ⁷ He gathered the waters of the sea upon each other;*ᶜ*
      He put up the *ocean* depths in reservoirs.*ᵈ*

⁸ Let all the earth fear the LORD;
Let all the inhabitants of the world stand in awe of him;
⁹ For
  He spoke, and it came to be;
  He commanded, and it stood firm.

¹⁰ The LORD
  Brings the plans of the *heathen* nations to nothing,
  And thwarts the plans of their people.
¹¹ The plans of the LORD *stand* for ever;
  The purposes of his heart stand through all generations.
¹² Blessed is
  The nation whose God is the LORD, and
  The people whom he has chosen as his inheritance.

¹³ The LORD looks down from heaven;
  He sees all the children of men;
  He looks upon all the inhabitants of the earth.
¹⁴ From his dwelling place
  He watches all the inhabitants of the earth.
    ¹⁵ He fashions the hearts of all of them;
      Thus, he understands all their works.

---

a   Or "shout."
b   Or "are done in faithfulness."
c   Or "into a heap."
d   Literally, "storehouses."

¹⁶ No king is saved by the size of his army;
  A warrior is not saved by his great strength; and
¹⁷ A horse is a false hope for victory
      As its great strength cannot deliver anyone.
¹⁸ But the eye of the LORD is
      On those who fear him;
      On those who hope on his unfailing love
        ¹⁹ To deliver their soul from death;
          And to keep them alive in famine.

²⁰ Our soul waits for the LORD,
      For he is our help and our shield.
    ²¹ For our heart rejoices in him,
      Because we trust in his holy name.

²² Let your lovingkindness, O LORD, be upon us
      Because we hope in you.

Psalm 34
Fear the Lord

A *psalm* of David.
Written when he changed his behavior^a before Abimelech; who drove him away
(and he left).

¹ I will bless the LORD at all times;
  His praise will always be in my mouth.
² My soul will boast *only* in the LORD;
      The humble will hear it and be glad.
³ Magnify the LORD with me;
  Let us exalt his name together.

⁴ I sought the LORD and he answered me, delivered me from all my fears.
⁵ Those who look to him are radiant; their faces are never ashamed.
⁶ This poor man cried,
      And the LORD heard him and saved him out of all his troubles.

⁷ The angel of the LORD encamps around those who fear him, and delivers them.
⁸ O taste and see that the LORD is good;
  Blessed is the man who takes refuge in him.

⁹ O fear the LORD, you his godly ones;
      For those who fear him lack nothing.
    ¹⁰ *Even* young lions lack *prey* and go hungry,
      But those who seek the LORD will not lack any good thing.

---

a   A reference to I Sam. 21:10-15, when David pretended he was insane.

¹¹ Come children, listen; and I'll teach you the fear of the LORD.
¹² Does any man amongst you
> Delight in life?
> Love *living* many days?
> *Hope* to see good *things?*

Here's how:
> ¹³ Keep your tongue from evil, your lips from deceitful talk;
> ¹⁴ Depart from evil;
> Do good;
> Seek peace, and pursue it.

¹⁵ The eyes of the LORD are upon the righteous,
> And his ears are listening for^a their cry.
¹⁶ The face of the LORD is against those who do evil,
> To cut off the memory of them from the earth.
¹⁷ The LORD hears when the righteous cry,
> And delivers them from all their troubles.
¹⁸ The LORD is close to the brokenhearted,
> And rescues those whose spirits are crushed.
¹⁹ The righteous *person* has many afflictions,
> But the LORD delivers him out of them all.
> ²⁰ He protects all his bones; not one will be broken.
²¹ Evil will slay the wicked,
> And those who hate the righteous will be condemned.
²² The LORD redeems the soul of his servants,
> And none of those who trust in him will be condemned.

Psalm 35
A Call for God's Protection

A psalm of David.

¹ LORD,
> Stand against those who stand against me;
> Fight against those who fight against me;
> ² Take up a body shield and an arm shield, rise up and help me;
> ³ Draw your spear and battle-axe^b against those who pursue me;
> Say to my soul, "I am your salvation."
> ⁴ Let those who seek after my life be disgraced and put to shame;
> Let those who plot evil against me be turned back and humiliated;
> ⁵ Let them be as chaff before the wind
>> With the angel of the LORD chasing them away;

---

a Literally, "toward."

b Or "and javelin."

⁶ Let their path be dark and slippery,
    With the angel of the LORD pursuing them; for
        ⁷ Without cause they hid their net, and
        Without cause they dug *a pit* for me.
⁸ Let destruction come upon them when they are unaware;
    Let the net they have hidden catch them;
    Let them fall to *their own* destruction.

⁹ Then my soul will rejoice in the LORD and exult in his salvation.
¹⁰ Every bone in my body*ᵃ* will say,
    "LORD, who is like you?
    Who *else* delivers
        The afflicted from those who are too strong for them,
        The poor and the needy from those who rob them?"

¹¹ Malicious witnesses
    Rise up and ask me about things of which I know nothing, ¹² and
    Repay me with evil for good, leaving my soul forlorn.
¹³ But as for me, when they were sick,
    My clothing was sackcloth;
    I humbled my soul with fasting;
        But my prayers *for them* returned unanswered;*ᵇ*
    ¹⁴ I went about as though *they had been* my friends or brothers;
    I bowed down as one mourning for his mother.
¹⁵ But when I limped,*ᶜ* they
    Gathered and rejoiced;
    Gathered against me like strangers—and I didn't know it!
    Slandered me without ceasing; and
    ¹⁶ Gnashed their teeth at me like godless mockers at a feast.

¹⁷ Lord,
    How long will you watch this?
    Rescue my soul from their ravaging, my life from these lions.
    ¹⁸ I will thank you in the great assembly;
    I will praise you before the crowds.*ᵈ*
    ¹⁹ Don't let those who are my enemies without cause rejoice over me;
    Don't let those who hate me without a cause wink their eye; for
        ²⁰ They do not speak of peace; but
        They devise deceitful words against those who are quiet in the land;
        ²¹ They open their mouths wide against me,
            Saying *falsely*, "Aha! Aha! Our eye has seen it."

---

a   Literally, "all my bones."
b   Literally, "returned into my bosom."
c   Or "stumbled."
d   Literally, "mighty throngs."

²² O LORD,
> You have seen it.

O Lord,
> Do not be silent;
> Do not be far from me;
> > ²³ Wake up!
> > Rise to my cause, to my judgment, my God and my Lord.

²⁴ O LORD,
> Judge me, my God, according to your righteousness; and
> Do not let them
> > Rejoice over me;
> > > ²⁵ Say in their hearts, "Ah, *we've got* our heart's desire";
> > > Say, "We have swallowed him up."

²⁶ Let those who rejoice about my troubles
> Be altogether confused and put to shame;

Let those who magnify themselves against me
> Be clothed with shame and dishonor;

²⁷ Let those who delight in my righteousness
> Shout for joy and be glad;
> Say continually,
> > "Great is the LORD, he who delights in the well-being*^a* of his servant."

²⁸ Then my tongue will tell of your righteousness and praise you all the day long.

Psalm 36
The Sin of the Wicked

A psalm of David, the servant of the Lord.
To the music director.

¹ Sin whispers to the wicked *deep* within his heart;
There is no fear of God before his eyes;
> ² For he flatters himself in his own eyes
> > Against discovering his own iniquity or God's*^b* hatred of it.*^c*

³ The words of his mouth are wicked and deceitful.
He has stopped being wise and doing good;
> ⁴ He plots evil while on his bed;
He sets himself in a path that is not good;
He does not reject evil.

---

a   Or "peace," or "prosperity." Hebrew: "shalom."
b   Literally, "his."
c   Or "that his iniquity will not be found out and hated."

The Mercy of the Lord

5 O LORD,
Your lovingkindness is in the heavens;
Your faithfulness *reaches* to the clouds;
6 Your righteousness is like the mighty mountains;
Your judgments are[a] like the great deep.
O LORD,
You preserve man and beast.

7 Your lovingkindness is so precious,[b] O God, *that* children of men:
Take refuge in the shadow of your wings;
8 Feast[c] on the abundance of your house; and
Drink from the river of your pleasures.
9 The fountain of life is with you;
We see light in your light.

10 Continue *giving*
Your lovingkindness to those who know you;
Your righteousness to the upright in heart.
11 Do not let the foot of the proud[d] come against me;
Do not let the hand of the wicked drive me away.

12 There, the workers of iniquity have fallen, cast down, unable to rise!

Psalm 37
Fret Not

A psalm of David.

1 Do not fret because of evildoers;
Do not be envious of the workers of iniquity;
2 For they will soon wither like the grass, fade away like green herbs.
3 Trust in the LORD and do good;
Dwell in the land,
Befriend[e] faithfulness.
4 Delight in the LORD and he will give you the desires of your heart.
5 Commit your way to the LORD—trust in him.
For he will act;
6 He will bring forth
Your righteousness as dawn, and
Your justice as the noonday *sun*.

---

a   Or "your justice is."
b   Or "how precious is your lovingkindness."
c   Literally, "drink their fill."
d   Or "of pride."
e   Or "cultivate."

⁷ Be still before the LORD—wait patiently for him *to act;*
 Do not fret
  Over those who prosper in their own way;
  Over men who carry out wicked schemes.
⁸ Let go of anger—forsake wrath—do not fret;
 For it leads only to evil, and ⁹ evildoers will be cut off.
 But those who wait upon the LORD will inherit the land.
  ¹⁰ For in a little while the wicked will not exist.*ᵃ*
   You will look at his place and he will be gone!*ᵇ*
  ¹¹ But the meek will inherit the land,
   And will delight themselves in the abundance of peace.*ᶜ*

¹² The wicked
  Plot against the righteous and
  Gnash their teeth at them.
   ¹³ The LORD laughs at them, for he sees that their day is coming.
¹⁴ The wicked
  Draw out their swords and bend their bows
   To cast down the poor and needy, and
   To slay those whose conduct is righteous;
¹⁵ But
  Their sword will stab their own heart; and
  Their bows will be broken.

¹⁶ Better is the little of the righteous than the abundance of many wicked.
  ¹⁷ For the strength*ᵈ* of the wicked will be broken,
 The LORD upholds the righteous;
¹⁸ The LORD knows the days of the blameless.
  Their inheritance will last*ᵉ* forever;
   ¹⁹ They will not be ashamed in evil times; and
 They will have an abundance in days of famine.

  ²⁰ Yes, the wicked will perish;
   The LORD's enemies will vanish like the glory of the fields, vanish like smoke.
    ²¹ *For* the wicked borrow and do not pay back,
     Whereas the righteous are generous and give.
  ²² For those who are blessed *by the LORD* will inherit the earth,
   And they who are cursed *by him* will be cut off.
²³ The steps of that man are made firm by the LORD when he delights in God's way.*ᶠ*
  ²⁴ Even if he stumbles, he will not fall down;
   For the LORD holds him up with his hand.

---

a Literally, "will not be."
b Literally, "will not be."
c Or "of prosperity," or "of well-being." Hebrew, "shalom."
d Literally, "arms."
e Literally, "be."
f Or "when God delights in his way." Literally, "when he delights in his way."

²⁵ I have been young, and now I am old;
   Yet have I not seen the righteous forsaken or their children begging for bread.
      ²⁶ They are generous and lend all day long;
         Their children are blessed.^a

²⁷ Turn from evil and do good;
      Then you will be secure^b forever.
²⁸ For the LORD loves justice;
   He will not forsake his godly ones.
      They will be preserved forever,
      But the children of the wicked will be cut off.
      ²⁹ The righteous will inherit the land and dwell in it forever.

³⁰ The mouth of the righteous speaks wisdom,
   And his tongue speaks about what is just.
³¹ The law of his God is in his heart;
   His steps do not slip.

³² The wicked watch for the righteous and seek to kill them.
³³ The LORD will not leave the righteous^c in their hand,
      Nor let them be condemned when they are brought to trial.

³⁴ Wait on the LORD;
   Keep his way.
      He will exalt you to inherit the land.
      You will see it when the wicked are cut off.

³⁵ I have seen a wicked and violent man spread himself like a luxuriant tree in its native soil,
³⁶ Yet he passed away, and, though I looked for him,^d he was no more.
   I looked for him, but he could not be found.

³⁷ Mark the blameless; look at the upright,
      For there is a future for the man of peace.
      ³⁸ But transgressors will be altogether destroyed;
         The future of the wicked will be cut off.
³⁹ The salvation of the righteous comes from the LORD;
   He is their stronghold in times of trouble.
⁴⁰ Because they take refuge in him,
   The LORD
      Helps them;
      Delivers them;
      Saves them;
      And rescues them from the wicked.

---

a Or "will be blessed," or "are a blessing."
b Literally, "dwell."
c Literally, "him."
d Literally, "yet he passes away, and, lo."

Psalm 38
Remember Me

A psalm of David. To cause to remember.

¹ O Lord,

　　Do not keep rebuking me in your anger;
　　Do not keep disciplining me in your wrath.
　　For
　　　² Your arrows have pierced me;
　　　　Your hand has come down on me;
　　　³ There is no soundness in my body because of your anger;
　　　　There is no health in my bones because of my sin.
　　　⁴ My iniquities are piled over my head, a heavy burden—too heavy.
　　　⁵ My wounds fester and stink because of my foolishness;
　　　⁶ I am bowed down, bent way over, and go about mourning all day long;
　　　⁷ My loins are filled with pain;*ᵃ*
　　　　There is nothing sound in my body;
　　　⁸ I am numb, completely crushed, groaning in my heart.

⁹ O Lord,

　　All my longings are before you;
　　My groans are not hidden;
　　¹⁰ My heart pounds;
　　My strength fails; and
　　Even the light of my eyes—it's gone!
　　¹¹ My loved ones and my friends stand back from my wounds.
　　　Even my family stands back, far away.
　　¹² Those who seek my life lay traps for me; and
　　Those who seek to hurt me talk *of my* destruction and plot deception all day
　　long.
　　¹³ But I,
　　　Like the deaf, do not listen *to them*;
　　　Like a mute, do not open my mouth;
　　　¹⁴ Have become like a man who does not hear, whose mouth corrects no
　　　one.*ᵇ*
　　¹⁵ For I am waiting for you, O LORD.
　　You will answer me, O Lord my God,

---

a Literally, "with burning."
b Literally, "has no reproofs."

16 For

I have prayed, "Do not let them who magnify themselves over me rejoice when my foot slips."

17 I am about to collapse[a]—my pain is constant.[b]

18 I will confess my iniquity—I am concerned about my sin.

19 My enemies are vigorous and strong;
Those who hate me without reason are numerous.
20 Those who repay good with evil oppose me,
Because I pursue what is good.
21 O LORD, do not forsake me;
My God, do not be far from me;
22 O Lord my savior, come quickly to help me.

Psalm 39
Prayer When Under Discipline

A psalm of David.
For Jeduthun, the music director.

1 I said *to myself*,
"I will guard my ways so I will not sin with my tongue;
I will muzzle my mouth when the wicked are in my presence."
2 I was mute—silent. I *even* refrained *from speaking* good,
And my sorrow grew.
3 My heart was hot within me;
A fire burned as I meditated;
So I prayed:[c]
4 "LORD,
Help me know my end, the number of my days, how many they are;
That I may know how fleeting my life *really* is.[d]
5 It's true,[e]
You have made my days merely the width of a hand; and
In your sight my lifetime is like *it is* nothing.
At its best, every man's *life* is only a mere breath *to you*. Selah
6 Man walks—but is only like a shadow *to you*;
He roars, but it's mere breath;
He piles up *riches*, but doesn't know who will end up with them.[f]

---

a Literally, "fall."
b Or "continually before me."
c Literally, "spoke with my tongue."
d Literally, "fleeting I am."
e Or "behold."
f Literally, "who will gather."

⁷ "And now, Lord,

    Why am I waiting? My hope is in you!
     ⁸ Deliver me from all my transgressions;
    Do not make me the reproach of the foolish.
   ⁹ Because you have done this *to me,* I have become silent, won't open my mouth.
   ¹⁰ I am exhausted from your hand opposing me;
   Remove your affliction from me.

   ¹¹ You discipline a man for his sin with rebukes;
   You consume his wealth like a moth.
   Surely every man is just mere breath.   Selah

¹² "O Lᴏʀᴅ,

    Hear my prayer;
    Listen to*ᵃ* my cry;
    Do not be silent *when you see* my tears;
     For I am your guest,*ᵇ* a visitor like my fathers *were.*

¹³ Turn from *disciplining* me so I can smile *again,* before I depart and am no more."

Psalm 40
Waiting, Praying and Trusting

A psalm of David.
To the music director.

 ¹ I waited patiently for the Lᴏʀᴅ, and
He
    Bent down to me and heard my cry;
   ² Brought me out of the pit of destruction,*ᶜ* the marshy bog;
   Set my feet upon a rock; and
   Made my steps secure.
³ He put a new song in my mouth, a song of praise to our God.
Many will see this, and will fear and put their trust in the Lᴏʀᴅ.

⁴ Blessed is that man who
    Makes the Lᴏʀᴅ his trust,
    Does not turn to the proud, to those who have swerved to what is not true.

⁵ O Lᴏʀᴅ my God,
    No one can compare to you;

---

a Literally, "give ear to."
b Literally, "a sojourner before you."
c Literally, "roaring pit."

Wonderful are your many deeds and thoughts toward us.[a]
I would proclaim them and talk about them, but they are too numerous to recount.

6 You've opened my ears.
You do not desire *only* sacrifices and offerings!
You do not require *just* burnt and sin offerings!
(7 When I realized this,[b] I said *to the Lord,* "Look, here I am[c]—*just as* it is recorded, written about me in the scroll. 8 I delight in doing your will, O my God. Your law is within my heart.")

9 I have proclaimed your righteousness[d] before the great congregation;
Look Lord, you know
I have not restrained my lips, and
10 I have not hidden your righteousness within my heart.
Rather,
I have spoken of your faithfulness and your salvation;
I have not concealed your lovingkindness and your truth from the great assembly.

11 O Lord,
Do not withhold your mercy from me;
Let your lovingkindness and your truth continually preserve me;
12 For
Innumerable troubles surround me;
My sins, more numerous than the hairs on my head, have overtaken me.
I am unable to see—my heart fails!
13 O Lord, deliver me;
O Lord, come quickly; help me.
Let those
14 Who seek after my life, *who seek* to destroy it, be totally confounded and put to shame;
Who wish me evil, be turned back and disgraced;
15 Who *falsely* say of me, "Aha! Aha!" be appalled by their shameful behavior;
16 Who seek you, rejoice and be glad in you;
Who love your salvation, continually say, "The Lord is great."

17 I am poor and needy, yet the Lord thinks of me!
You are my help and my deliverer.
O my God, do not delay.

---

a   Or "and plans for us."
b   Literally, "at that time."
c   Or "I come."
d   Or "justice."

Psalm 41
Considering the Poor

A psalm of David.
To the music director.

¹ Whoever considers the poor is blessed.
The LORD will
>> Deliver him in times of trouble;
>> ² Preserve him and keep him alive;
>> Bless him in the land;
>> Not give him up to the will of his enemies;
>> ³ Sustain him on his sickbed; and
>> Restore him to health when he is ill.^{*a*}

Praying for Mercy

⁴ I prayed,
>> "LORD, have mercy on me;
>> Heal me;
>>> For I have sinned against you.

⁵ "My enemies ask maliciously,
>> 'When will he die, his name disappear?'
⁶ When one comes to see me,
>> He speaks falsely while his heart gathers slander;^{*b*}
When he leaves,
>> He tells them on the street.
⁷ All who hate me whisper together against me, hoping evil for me,
Saying,
>> ⁸ 'Let an evil disease come upon him.
>> When he lies down, let him not get up again.'
⁹ Even my close friend, whom I trusted, who ate my food, has lifted his heel against me.

¹⁰ "But you, O LORD,
>> Are gracious to me;
>> Raise me up that I may repay them.
¹¹ By this I know
>> That you are pleased with me;
>> That my enemy will not shout *in triumph* over me; and
>> ¹² That you uphold my integrity^{*c*} and have set me in your presence forever."

---

a Literally, "turn over his bed in his illness."
b Literally, "wickedness."
c Or "you uphold me due to my integrity."

Closing Doxology

¹³ Blessed be the LORD, the God of Israel,
From everlasting to everlasting.
Amen and Amen.

BOOK TWO

Psalm 42
The Downcast Soul I

To the music director.
A maskil of the sons of Korah.

¹ As the deer yearns for streams of water,
So my soul yearns for you, O God.

² My soul thirsts for God, the living God.
When will I *be able to* go and appear before God?
³ My tears have been my food day and night while people*ᵃ* ask me, "Where is your God?"
⁴ As I pour out my soul, I remember the *good* times;
Going with the crowd of *worshippers*;
And leading them to the house of God with the voice of joy and praise—what a multitude kept the holyday!
⁵ *So*, O my Soul,
Why are you downcast?
Why the turmoil within me?
Hope in God,
For I will again praise him for his rescuing presence.*ᵇ*

⁶ O my God,
My soul is downcast within me,
So I will remember you *when I am:*
In the land of Jordan;
On the Hermonites;*ᶜ*
On the small hills;*ᵈ*
⁷ Where the deep oceans call deeply,
By the noisy waterfalls, or
Wherever all your waves and breakers sweep over me.

---

a   Literally, "they."
b   Literally, "the salvation of his face."
c   Mt. Hermon and the high mountains around it, about thirty miles north of the Sea of Galilee.
d   Or "Mt. Mizar." "Mizar" means "small."

[8] By day the LORD directs his lovingkindness *toward me*;
  At night his song, my prayer to the God of my life, is with me.
[9] I cry to God my Rock:
    "Why have you forgotten me"
    "Why do I go about mourning oppressed by the enemy who
      [10] Taunts me;
    Shakes[a] my bones; and
    Asks all day long, 'Where is your God?'"

[11] O my soul,
    Why are you downcast?
    Why the turmoil within me?
    Hope in God.
      For I will again praise him, my God, for his rescuing presence.[b]

Psalm 43
The Downcast Soul II

[1] Vindicate me, O God;
  Plead my cause against an ungodly nation;
  Deliver me from deceitful and unjust men.
[2] You are God, my fortress.
    Why have you rejected me?
    Why do I go about mourning, oppressed by my enemy?
[3] Send your light and your truth.
    Let them lead me;
    Let them bring me to your holy hill, to your dwelling.
[4] Then
    I will go to your altar, O God;
    I will go to you, God, *the source of* my overflowing joy; and
    I will praise you on the harp, O God, my God.

[5] O my soul,
    Why are you downcast?
    Why the disturbance within me?
    Hope in God,
      For I will again praise him, my God, for his rescuing presence.[c]

---

a Literally, "shatters."
b Literally, "the salvation of his face."
c Literally, "the salvation of his face."

Psalm 44
Israel's Lament

To the music director.
A maskil of the sons of Korah.

¹ We have heard with our ears, O God;
Our fathers told us the wonders you did in their days, the days of old:
² *How* you drove out the *heathen* nations with your hand;
How you planted our fathers;[a]
How you broke the *heathen* peoples into pieces and sent them away.
³ For our fathers[b]
Did not take possession of the land by sword and
Did not save themselves by their own arm;
But *were saved* by your right hand, your arm, your presence;[c]
Because you favored them.

⁴ You are my king, O God;
Command victories for Jacob.
⁵ Through you we will push back our enemies;
Through your name we will trample those who rise against us.
⁶ We will trust neither our bows nor our swords to save us;[d]
⁷ For you have saved us from our enemies, put to shame those who hated us.
⁸ In God we boast all the day long, praising your name forever.　　Selah

⁹ But now you have:
Rejected us,
Put us to shame,
Not gone out with our armies,
¹⁰ Made us retreat from our enemy—and those who hate us have plundered us.

¹¹ You have:
Set us up to be eaten like sheep,
Scattered us among the *heathen* nations,
¹² Sold your people for a pittance—getting little[e] from their sale,
¹³ Made us the laughing stock[f] of our neighbors—scorned and derided by those around us, and
¹⁴ Made us a well-known example[g] among the *heathen* nations—who[h] shake their heads at us.[i]

---

a　Literally, "planted them."
b　Literally, "they."
c　Literally, "the light of your face."
d　Though in the first person singular in Hebrew, we present this verse in the first person plural due to the context.
e　Literally, "not becoming much."
f　Literally, "reproach," or "taunt."
g　Literally, "made us a proverb."
h　Literally, "those people."
i　Literally, "at our people."

¹⁵ My humiliation is continually before me;
  The shame on my face overwhelms me
    ¹⁶ When I hear their reproaches and blasphemy,^{*a*}
    When I see our vengeful enemies.
¹⁷ All this has happened though we have neither forgotten you nor violated^{*b*} your covenant.
¹⁸ Our heart has not turned away *from you*;
  Nor have our steps departed from your path
    ¹⁹ Though you have broken us in this place of jackals and covered us with the shadow *of death*.
      (²⁰ If we had forgotten the name of our God or stretched out our hands to a foreign god, ²¹ would not you, a God who knows the secrets of the heart, have discovered it?)
²² Yet for your sake
  We face death^{*c*} all day long;
  We are regarded as sheep *destined* for slaughter.

²³ Wake up, Lord! Why do you sleep?
  Get up! Do not cast us off forever.
²⁴ Why do you hide your face and forget we are afflicted and oppressed?
²⁵ Our souls have sunk down to the dust;
  Our bodies cling to the ground.
²⁶ Arise, help us, redeem us because of your lovingkindness.

Psalm 45
A Subject's Note to His King and Queen^{*d*}

To the music director: to the tune of "The Lilies."
A love song^{*e*} *and* a maskil of the sons of Korah.

A personal note from the psalmist: ¹ My heart overflows on this beautiful theme. I am addressing my verses to the king. My tongue is *like* the pen of a skillful writer, *declaring*:

² You are the most handsome of the sons of men;
  Grace has anointed^{*f*} your lips;
  And so, God has blessed you forever.
³ Strap your sword upon your thigh, O mighty one;
  Clothe yourself in splendor and majesty;

---

a "Blasphemy": an act or spoken word showing disrespect for God.
b Literally, "dealt falsely with."
c Literally, "are killed."
d Perhaps for the king's coronation.
e Or "wedding song."
f Literally, "been poured upon."

4 Ride in your majesty, victoriously for the cause of truth, humility and
righteousness.
>Let your right hand teach awesome things;
>5 Let your sharp arrows *pierce* the hearts of the king's enemies;
>>Let *the heathen* nations fall beneath you.
6 Your throne, O God-like one,[a] is forever and ever.
Your kingship's scepter is a scepter of righteousness,
>7 For you love righteousness and hate wickedness.
Therefore:
>God, your god, has anointed you over your companions with the oil of joy;
>8 All your robes smell of myrrh and aloes and cassia;
>The music of strings from ivory palaces makes you glad;
>9 Daughters of kings are among your noble women;
>The queen stands at your right hand in gold from Ophir.

Counsel for the Queen

10 O royal daughter, listen, consider, pay attention[b] *to my counsel*:
>Forget about your people and your father's house;
>11 Let the king desire[c] your beauty;
>Since he is your lord, bow to him.
>12 Daughter of Tyre, *even* the richest people will seek your favor.[d]

---

13 The princess, so glorious within *her chamber* with clothing interwoven with gold, 14 will be brought before the king in embroidered *robes.*
Her virgin companions will follow and be brought to you, 15 brought with joy and gladness as they enter into the king's palace.
16 Your children will take the positions[e] of their fathers;
>You will make your children[f] princes throughout the land.

17 I will cause your name to be remembered throughout all generations,
>Therefore the people[g] will praise you forever and ever.

---

a Literally, "God." The psalmist sees the royal groom in all his splendor as like God. Hebrews 1:8 shows that this is also a reference to Jesus Christ.
b Literally, "incline your ear."
c Or "the king desires."
d The Hebrew is not clear.
e Literally, "place."
f Literally, "them."
g Or "the nations."

Psalm 46
God Is Our Refuge and Our Strength

To the music director.
A psalm of the sons of Korah. *According to* alamoth.[a]

^{1} God is our refuge and strength,
  An ever-present help in *times of* trouble.
^{2} That is why we will not fear
  Though the earth give way;
  Though the mountains slip into the midst[b] of the sea;
   ^{3} Though waters *of the seas* roar and foam;
  Though the mountains are shaken by the waves of the sea.[c]   Selah

^{4} There is a river whose streams make glad the city of God,
  The holy place where the Most High dwells.
   ^{5} God is in the midst of the city;[d] she will not be moved.
  God will help her when morning dawns.

^{6} *When heathen* nations rage, kingdoms totter!
But when God[e] raises his voice, the earth melts!
^{7} The LORD almighty[f] is with us;
  The God of Jacob is our refuge.   Selah

 God says
^{8} "Come and see the works of the LORD
  Who has brought destructions upon the earth,
   ^{9} Who has made wars cease all over[g] of the earth,
  Who breaks bows, snaps[h] spears and burns chariots with fire.
^{10} Be still!
Know that I am God!
  I will be exalted among the nations;
  I will be exalted throughout the earth."

^{11} The LORD of hosts is with us;
  The God of Jacob is our refuge.   Selah

---

a "Alamoth": an undefined musical or liturgical term, or a tune or musical instrument.
b Literally, "heart."
c Literally, "mountains quake with the swelling thereof."
d Literally, "her."
e Literally, "he."
f Or "Lord of hosts."
g Literally, "to the ends."
h Literally, "shatter."

Psalm 47
Clap and Sing Praises

To the music director.
A psalm of the sons of Korah.

¹ Clap your hands, all you people;
Shout to God with cries*a* of joy;
² For

The LORD most high, the great King over all the earth, is to be feared;
³ He will subdue the people under us, *place the heathen* nations under our feet!
⁴ He chose our inheritance for us, the pride of Jacob, whom he loves!   Selah
⁵ God has ascended with a shout;
The LORD *has ascended* with the sound of a trumpet.

⁶ Sing praises to God—Sing praises.
Sing praises to our King—Sing praises;
⁷ For God is the King of all the earth.
Sing a maskil;
For

⁸ God reigns over the *heathen* nations;
God sits on his holy throne;
⁹ The princes of the people gather along with the people of the God of
Abraham,
For the shields of the earth *belong* to God.
He is highly exalted.

Psalm 48
Celebrating Jerusalem

A song and psalm for the sons of Korah.

¹ Great is the LORD, and to be praised greatly in the city of our God, on his holy
mountain.

² Beautiful in *its* elevation!   The joy of all the earth!
MT. ZION

In the far north!   The city of the great King!

³ Within her fortified towers, God is known as her stronghold.
⁴ For instance,*b* when kings assembled and marched*c* together, ⁵ they saw
the city*d* and were astounded and fled—terrified! ⁶ Panic*e* seized them, and
they anguished like a woman in labor. ⁷ *The Lord* destroyed them *like* ships

---

a Literally, "the voice."
b Literally, "for behold."
c Literally, "passed by."
d Literally, "it."
e Or "trembling."

of Tarshish *destroyed by* an east wind. ⁸*Just as* we have heard, and now have seen: in the city of the LORD of Hosts, the city of our God, God makes her secure forever.
Selah

⁹ While *worshipping* in the midst of your temple, we reflect on your lovingkindness, O God.
¹⁰ Like your name, O God,
>Your praise *reaches* to the ends of the earth;
>Your right hand is filled with righteousness.
¹¹ Let Mount Zion rejoice;
Let the daughters of Judah rejoice because of your judgments.

¹² Walk around *the city of* Zion.
>Walk about her;
>Count her towers;
>>¹³ Consider her fortified walls;
>>Go through her remarkable buildings*ᵃ*
So you can tell the next generation *about it.*
¹⁴ For this God is our God forever and ever;
He will be our guide forever.

Psalm 49
The Futility of Wealth

To the music director.
A psalm of the sons of Korah.

¹ Hear this, all you people;
Listen, all you inhabitants of the world—²both high and low, rich and poor, *all* together.
>³ My mouth will speak wisdom;
>The meditation of my heart *will ponder* understanding;
>⁴ I will turn my ear to proverbs to solve*ᵇ* my perplexing questions
>>*While listening to the music* of the harp.
>⁵ Why should I be afraid in *these* days of adversity when the iniquity of my foes surrounds me?

⁶ About those who trust in their wealth and boast of their great riches:
>⁷ No man can by any means redeem *the soul* of another,*ᶜ* give God a ransom for it ⁸ so that he will live eternally *on earth* and not see the pit.
>>⁹ For the redemption of a soul is *too* costly, so he should cease *trying* forever.
¹⁰ Anyone*ᵈ* can see that:
>The wise die and leave their wealth to others;

---

a   Or "citadels. Literally, "palaces,"."
b   Literally, "open."
c   Or "his brother."
d   Literally, "they."

They die just like the foolish and senseless *die*;

11 Their inner thought is that
>> Their households will continue*a* forever, and
>> Their dwellings will be left for*b* all *their future* generations.
> They have *even* named their lands after their own names!

12 But
>> No man will remain*c* in his pomp;
>> They are like the beasts that perish;

13 Their way is their foolishness,
>>> As is that of those who follow and agree with their words.

14 Like sheep they are destined*d* for the grave—death will feed on them;
>> The upright will rule over them in the morning;
>> Their forms will be consumed in Sheol *far from* their dwellings.

15 But God will redeem my soul from the power of Sheol;
> He will receive me.   Selah

16 So do not be overwhelmed*e* when *a person* becomes rich and the glory of his house increases.

17 For when he dies
> He will carry nothing away;
> His honors will not descend with him

18 Even though
>> While he lived he congratulated himself,*f* and
>> Men praised him for doing well.

19 He will join*g* the generation of his fathers—who will never see light.

20 Self-important men who do not have understanding are like the beasts that perish.

Psalm 50
Offer Praise and Order Your Life

A psalm of Asaph.

1 The Mighty One, God, the LORD, speaks and summons the earth from the rising of the sun to its setting.

2 God shines forth from Zion, the perfection of beauty.

3 Our God approaches*h* and will not keep silent;

---

a Literally, "are."
b Literally, "dwellings are to."
c Literally, "man will not remain."
d Literally, "are appointed to."
e Literally, "afraid."
f Or "counted himself blessed."
g Literally, "go to."
h Literally, "comes."

Fire devours before him and storms *rage* all around him,
  ⁴ That he may judge his people.
He calls to the heavens above and the earth, *saying,*
  ⁵ "Bring me^a my faithful ones, those who have made a covenant by sacrifice."

⁶ The heavens proclaim his righteousness.
God himself is judge, *and says:*   Selah
  ⁷ "Hear, O my people, and I will speak;
  Hear, O Israel, and I will testify against you.
  I am God, your God.

  ⁸ "I will not rebuke you for your sacrifices or your burnt offerings which are
  always before me.
  ⁹ I will not accept a bull from your stall^b or a goat from your pens,
    ¹⁰ For every beast of the forest is mine;
    The cattle upon a thousand hills *are mine;*
      ¹¹ I know every bird of the mountains;
      Everything that moves in the field is mine—¹² if I were hungry, I would not
      tell you;
      The world is mine, and everything that is in it.
  ¹³ *And, really,* do I eat the flesh of bulls, or drink goat's blood?

  ¹⁴ "Offer to *your* God an offering of thanksgiving, and
  Perform your vows to the Most High.
  ¹⁵ *Then* call upon me in the day of trouble.
  Then I will deliver you, and you will glorify me."

¹⁶ But God says to the wicked:
  "What *right* do you have to recite my statutes, to put my covenant on your
  lips?
  ¹⁷ You
        Hate discipline;^c
        Cast my words behind you;
      ¹⁸ Join thieves when you see them;
        Associate with adulterers;
      ¹⁹ Give your mouth to evil, frame deceit with your tongue; and
      ²⁰ Sit and speak against your brother—slander your *own* mother's son!
  ²¹ You have done these things, and I have kept silent.
  You thought that I was just like you,
        But *now* I will rebuke you
        And state my case^d before your eyes.

---

a Literally, "gather to me.".
b Literally, "house." In ancient times there were stalls in the same building in which the family lived.
c Or "hate my discipline."
d Literally, "and set it in order."

²² "Now consider this, you who forget God, otherwise I will tear you in pieces
and no one *will be able* to deliver you:
²³ Whoever sacrifices offerings of thanksgiving glorifies me.
I will show the salvation of God to whoever sets his path *aright.*"

Psalm 51
Psalm of the Penitent

A psalm of David.
To the music director.

Written after Nathan the prophet came in him after he had gone in to Bathsheba.

¹ Have mercy upon me, O God,
According to your lovingkindness, your great compassion;
Blot out my transgressions;
² Wash me thoroughly from my iniquity;
Cleanse me from my sin;
³ For I know my transgressions,
And my sin is always before me.
⁴ Against you, you only, have I sinned and done what is evil in your sight;
So you are justified when you speak, blameless when you judge.
⁵ Surely I was born*ᵃ* in iniquity—in sin my mother conceived me.
⁶ Nevertheless,*ᵇ* you desire truth in the innermost being;
Teach me wisdom there.*ᶜ*

⁷ Purge me with hyssop,*ᵈ* and I will be clean;
Wash me, and I will be whiter than snow.
⁸ Let me hear joy and gladness *again;*
Let the bones which you have broken rejoice.
⁹ Hide your face from my sins, and
Blot out all my iniquities.
¹⁰ Create in me a clean heart, O God; and
Renew a right spirit within me.

¹¹ Do not cast me away from your presence, and
Do not take your holy spirit from me.
¹² Restore to me the joy of your salvation, and
Sustain me with a spirit that will obey you;*ᵉ*
¹³ Then I will teach transgressors your ways,
And sinners will turn back to you.

---

a   Literally, "brought forth."
b   Literally, "behold."
c   Literally, "in what is hidden"; or "in the hidden part."
d   "Hyssop": a plant priests used to dip into blood and sprinkle it.
e   Literally, "with a willing spirit."

[14] O God, God of my salvation,
>> Deliver me from the guilt of murder;[a]
>> And my tongue will sing aloud of your righteousness.
[15] O Lord,
>> Open my lips, and my mouth will praise you.[b]

[16] You do not want[c] a sacrifice, or I would give it;
> You are not pleased by burnt offerings.
[17] The sacrifices of God are
>> A broken spirit;
>> A broken and repentant heart.
> O God, you will not despise these.

[18] Do good to Zion in your good pleasure;
> Build up the walls of Jerusalem.
[19] Then you will delight in righteous sacrifices—in burnt offerings—and whole burnt offerings.
> Then bulls will be offered on your altar.

Psalm 52
David's Grief When Saul Murdered the Priests of the Lord

A maskil of David.
To the music director.

Written after Doeg the Edomite went to speak to Saul and told him, "David has come to the house of Ahimelech."[d]

[1] Why brag about your evil deeds, O mighty man?
>> The lovingkindness of God protects me every day.[e]
[2] Your tongue devises disasters;
>> It's a sharp razor, a deceitful worker.
[3] You love evil more than good, lying more than speaking truth;   Selah
[4] You love all the words that devour, you liar.[f]
[5] God will
>> Bring you down permanently;
>> Snatch you up and tear you from your tent; and
>> Uproot you from the land of the living.   Selah
[6] The righteous will see, then fear and laugh *and say:*
>> [7] "Look at the man
>>> Who would not make God his fortress;
>>> Who trusted in the abundance of his riches; and

---

a Literally, "bloodguiltiness."
b Literally, "declare your praise."
c Or "delight in"
d See I Sam. 22:9.
e Literally, "is every day."
f Literally, "deceitful tongue."

Who grew strong by destroying others." [a]

8 As for me,
    I am like a green olive tree in the house of God;
    I trust in the lovingkindness of God forever and ever.

Lord,
  9 I will praise you forever,
    Because you have done it *before;*
    I will wait, *calling* on your name in the presence of the godly;
      For that is good.

Psalm 53
The Fool

A maskil of David.
To the music director: according to mahalath. [b]

1 The fool says in his heart, "There is no God."
    Such people [c] are corrupt;
    They do abominable [d] deeds;
    Not one *of them* does good.

2 God looks down from heaven at the children of men to see if there is anyone who
understands, who seeks God;
3 But everyone has turned aside;
    Together they have become corrupt;
    There is no one who does good—not even one!

4 Don't the workers of iniquity have *any* knowledge,
    Those who eat up my people just as they eat bread?
    Those who have not called upon God?

Future Judgment of the Wicked

5 There they are in great fear where no fear was, *except that*
    God scattered the bones of those who besieged his people. [e]
    His people put the wicked [f] to shame, because God despised
    them.

---

6 Oh that the salvation of Israel would come out of Zion *now.*
  When God restores his *captive* [g] people, Jacob will rejoice; Israel will be glad.

---

a Literally, "was strong in his destruction."
b "Mahalath": an undefined musical or liturgical term, or a tune or musical instrument.
c Literally, "they."
d "Abominable": extremely repugnant, offensive.
e Literally, "encamped against them."
f Literally, "they put them."
g *"Captive,"* from Ps. 14:7.

Psalm 54
David in Distress

A maskil of David.
To the music director: with stringed instruments.
Written after the Ziphites went to Saul and said, "Isn't David hiding among us?"[a]

¹ O God,
>Save me by your name;
>Defend me with your might.
² O God,
>Hear my prayer;
>Listen to the words of my mouth,
>>³ For strangers have risen up against me.
>>Ruthless men seek my life.
>>They have no regard for God.[b]   Selah

⁴ Surely,
>God is my helper;
>The Lord is the sustainer of my life;
>⁵ He will repay my enemies for *their* evil.

O God,
>Destroy them as you promised.[c]
>⁶ I will sacrifice a freewill offering to you;
>I will praise your name, O LORD,
>>For It is good;
>>⁷ For you have delivered me from all trouble; and
>>My eyes have looked in triumph over my enemies.[d]

Psalm 55
Psalm of the Troubled

A maskil of David.
To the music director: with stringed instruments.

¹ O God,
>Listen to my prayer; don't hide from my plea;
>² Hear me; answer me.
>I am restless about my complaint—moaning
>>³ Because of the threats[e] of the enemy, the pressure of the wicked.
>>They rain trouble upon me, angrily bear a grudge against me.
>⁴ My heart within me is in anguish;

---

a   See I Sam. 23:19
b   Literally, "they have not set God before them."
c   Literally, "in your faithfulness."
d   Literally, "have looked in triumph on my enemies."
e   Literally, "voice."

Terrors of death have fallen upon me;
5 Fear and trembling have come upon me; and
Horror has overwhelmed me.

6 So I say:
"Oh, that I had wings like a dove!
I would fly away and be at rest;
7 Yes, I would wander far off and stay in the wilderness;   Selah
8 I would hurry to find shelter from this raging wind, this gale."

9 Confuse *the wicked*, O Lord;
Divide their tongues,
Because I have seen *their* violence and strife in the city.
10 Day and night they prowl[a] her walls·
Trouble and sorrow are within it;
11 Destruction is in her midst;
Deceit and oppression never leave her streets.

David's Deceitful Companion, Part I.

12 It is not an enemy who reproaches me;
If it were, I could bear it.
Nor is it *someone* who hates me and exalts himself *by speaking* against me.
If it were, I could hide from him.
13 But it is you! One of us![b] My companion! My friend!
14 We had close fellowship walking with the throng in the house of God!

---

15 Let death seize them!
Let them go down into Sheol—alive!
For evil is in their dwellings and among them.

16 As for me:
I will call upon God;
The LORD will save me;
17 Evening, morning and at noon I will complain—cry out *until* he hears my voice.
18 Though many are *still* against me, he will ransom[c] my life to safety[d] from the battle waged against me,
19 God, enthroned from old, will hear and afflict[e] them,   Selah
Because they will not change, will not fear God.

---

a Literally, "go around."
b Literally, "a man my equal."
c Or "redeem."
d Or "peace."
e Or "humble."

---

*David's Deceitful Companion, **Part II**.*

²⁰ My companion*ᵃ* struck out*ᵇ* against his friends.*ᶜ* He broke his covenant. ²¹ His speech was smooth as butter, but war was in his heart. His words were softer than oil, yet they *cut like* drawn swords.

---

²² Cast your burden upon the LORD; he will sustain you;
He will never permit the righteous to be moved.

²³ O God,

You will send the wicked*ᵈ* down into the pit of destruction.
Bloodthirsty and deceitful men will not live out half their days.
But I trust in you.

Psalm 56
David Calls for Help and Trusts God.

A miktam of David.
To the music director: to the tune of "The Dove on Distant Oaks."
Written when the Philistines seized him at Gath.

¹ O God,

Be merciful to me.
Men are trampling upon me, fighting me all day long, oppressing me.
² My enemies trample me all day long;
Many fight against me.
³ When I am afraid, I will trust
⁴ In God, whose word I praise;
In God, whom I trust.
I will not be afraid—what can *mere* flesh do to me?

⁵ All day long they distort my words;
All their thoughts are against me and for evil.
⁶ They abide together, lurking, watching my steps, waiting to take my life.
⁷ Cast them out because of their wickedness;*ᵉ*
In your anger, bring down these people.*ᶠ*

⁸ You have kept count of my sorrows, put my tears in your bottle—aren't they *recorded* in your book?
⁹ Therefore, my enemies will turn back on the day I call *for help.*
This I know: God is for me:

---

a   Literally, "he."
b   Literally, "he used his hands."
c   Literally, "those who were at peace with him."
d   Literally, "them."
e   Or "will they escape despite their wickedness?"
f   Literally, "the peoples."

¹⁰ God, whose word I praise;
    The L<small>ORD</small>, whose word I praise;
¹¹ God, whom I trust.
I will not be afraid—what can man do to me?

¹² I must fulfill my vows to you, God;
    So I will render thank offerings to you.
¹³ For you have delivered my soul from death and my feet from stumbling,
    That I may walk before you, God, in the light of life.

Psalm 57
Praising God in the Midst of Trouble

A miktam of David.
To the music director: to the tune of "Do Not Destroy."
Regarding his flight from Saul into the cave.

¹ Have mercy, O God, have mercy on me;
    For my soul takes refuge in you.
    I take refuge in the shadow of your wings
        Until the danger^{*a*} passes by.

² I cry to God Most High, to the God who fulfills *his purpose* for me.^{*b*}
³ He will
    Send *help* from heaven, and
    Deliver me from those who reproach me and pant after me.   Selah
God will send forth his lovingkindness and his truth.

⁴ My soul is in the midst of lions;
  I lie among those who breathe fire, sons of men
    Whose teeth are arrows and spears;
    Whose tongues are sharp swords.

⁵ O God
    Be exalted above the heavens;
    Let your glory *shine* over all the earth.

  ⁶ They have set a net for my feet—my soul is bowed down.
    They have dug a pit in front of me and fallen into it!   Selah

    ⁷ My heart is steadfast, O God;
    My heart is steadfast;
    I will sing—sing praises.
      ⁸ Wake up, my glory;^{*c*}
        Wake up, psaltery and harp.
    I will awaken the dawn.

---

a   Literally, "destruction."

b   Or "accomplishes *his purpose* through me."

c   "Glory": a symbolic reference, perhaps to his tongue or soul.

⁹ I will praise thee, O Lord, among the people;
I will sing about you among the nations;
¹⁰ For your lovingkindness is great, reaching to the heavens;
And your faithfulness reaches the clouds.

¹¹ Be exalted, O God, *even* above the heavens!
Let your glory be over all the earth.

Psalm 58
Confidence That God Will Judge the Wicked

A miktam of David.
To the music director: *to the tune of* "Do Not Destroy."

¹ Indeed,
Do you rulers speak righteously?
Do you judge the children of men uprightly?
² No!
In your hearts you devise wickedness;
Your hands spread violence on the earth.

³ The wicked
Are estranged *from God* from the womb;
Go astray at birth;
And speak lies.
⁴ Their poison is like the venom of a snake;
Like that of a deaf cobra[a] that stops up its ears (⁵ as a result it does not hear
the voice of *its master*—the *snake* charmer, *even* a skillful charmer.)
⁶ O God,
Break their teeth in their mouths.
O Lord,
Break off the fangs of the young lions.
⁷ Let them vanish[b] like water that runs off;
Cut them off when they pull back their arrows.[c]
⁸ Let them pass away like a snail that melts,[d] like a woman's miscarriage—
never to see the sun.
⁹ Sweep them away before their *cooking* pots can feel *the heat of* green, or *even*
dry, thorns.

¹⁰ The righteous will rejoice when they see *his* vengeance;
They will bathe their feet in the blood of the wicked.
¹¹ Then men will say:
"Truly there is a reward for the righteous.
Surely there is a God who judges the earth."

---

a Snakes are deaf to sounds travelling through the air.
b Literally, "flow away."
c The Hebrew of this line is unclear.
d Picture how a snail seems to be melting as it leaves its slime behind it.

Psalm 59
A Call for Deliverance

A miktam of David *regarding* when Saul sent *men* to watch his house to kill him.
To the music director: *to the tune of* "Do Not Destroy."

[1] O my God,
    Deliver me from my enemies;
    Protect me from those who rise up against me;
    [2] Deliver me from those who do evil; and
    Save me from bloodthirsty men.
    [3] Look!
      They lie in wait for me;
      Fierce men conspire against me;
        Not due to my transgression,
        Not due to my sin, O LORD.
     [4] They run and prepare themselves.
    It's not my fault—arise–help me–look!

[5] O LORD God of hosts, God of Israel,
    Rise up and punish all the *heathen* nations;
    Have no mercy on any of these wicked transgressors who   Selah
     [6] Return at evening;
     Prowl around the city snarling like dogs. [7] Look, they
     Belch *filth* from their mouths, swords from their lips; and
     Say, "Who can hear us?"

[8] O LORD,
    Laugh at them;
    Scoff at all these *heathen* nations.
[9] O My Strength,
    I am waiting[a] for you.
O God,
    You are my fortress,
   [10] The steadfast God[b] who will go before me;
    You, God, will let me look in triumph upon my enemies.

[11] Don't kill them, or my people will forget;
Instead:
    Just scatter them by your power;
    Bring them down, O Lord our shield;
   [12] Let them be taken in their pride;
     For the sin of their mouth, the words of their lips, the curses and lies
     they utter.

---

a Literally, "watching."
b Or "the God of lovingkindness."

[13] *No!* Destroy them in your wrath—destroy them until they no longer exist![a]
Let it be known to the ends of the earth that God rules in Jacob.   Selah

[14] *No!* Let them return this evening;
Let them prowl about the city snarling like dogs;
[15] Let them wander about for food and growl if they are not satisfied.
[16] Then I will sing about your power;
Yes, I will sing joyfully about your lovingkindness in the morning,
For you are my fortress, my refuge in times[b] of trouble.

[17] O my strength,
I will sing to you;
For you, O God, are my fortress, my steadfast God.[c]

Psalm 60
A Plea for Restoration

A miktam of David for instruction.
To the music director: *to the tune of* "The Lily of the Covenant."[d]

Written regarding when he fought *the Syrian army led by* Aram Naharaim and Aram Zobah, and *when* Joab returned after defeating twelve thousand Edomites in the Valley of Salt.

[1] O God,
You have rejected us, broken us and been angry *with us;*
Now restore us.
[2] You have shaken the earth and torn it open;
Now seal the cracks, for it still quakes.
[3] You have shown your people hard times;
You have given us wine to drink that makes us stagger.
[4] But you have set up a rallying flag for those who fear you,
That they might flee to it from the bow.   Selah
[5] Save us with your right hand;
Answer us so your beloved may be delivered.

[6] God, you *once* spoke in your holiness,[e] *saying:*
"In triumph I will divide up Shechem and measure off the valley of Succoth.

---

a Literally, "until they are no more."
b Literally, "the day of."
c Literally, "God of lovingkindness."
d Or "Lily of the Testimony."
e Or "from your sanctuary."

⁷ Gilead and Manasseh are mine;
   Ephraim is my chief stronghold;*ᵃ*
   Judah is my scepter;
⁸ Moab is my washpot;
   I will throw my shoe*ᵇ* at Edom, and
   I will shout in triumph over Philistia."
⁹ *But now*—who will bring me into the fortified city, lead me into Edom?
¹⁰ God, haven't you rejected us?
  God, you don't go out with our armies.
¹¹ Oh *God*, give us help against our enemies,
    For deliverance by man is vanity.

¹² With God we will act boldly,
   For he will trample down our foes.

Psalm 61
Trust in God

A psalm of David.
To the music director: with stringed instruments.

¹ O God,
   Hear my cry; listen to my prayer.
    ² *I will go* to the ends of the earth to cry to you,
      Because my heart is overwhelmed.
   Lead me to a *sheltering* rock that is higher than I am;
    ³ For you have been a refuge for me, a strong tower against the enemy.
  ⁴ Let me dwell in your tent forever;
   Let me take refuge in the shelter of your wings;   Selah
  ⁵ For you, O God,
    Have heard my vows; and
    Have given me the heritage of those who fear your name.
  ⁶ Prolong the king's life—may his years *span* many generations.
  ⁷ Let him reign*ᶜ* before God forever;
   Provide*ᵈ your* lovingkindness and faithfulness to preserve*ᵉ* him.

⁸ Then I will sing praises to your name as I fulfill my vows day by day.

---

a Or "helmet."
b "Throw my shoe": an insulting gesture.
c Literally, "be enthroned."
d Literally, "appoint."
e Or "watch over."

Psalm 62
Waiting for God

A psalm of David.
For Jeduthun, the music director.

¹ My soul waits in silence for God alone.
   My salvation comes from him;
      ² He alone is my rock, my salvation, my defense;
      I will not be shaken.

³ How long will *wicked people* assault me[a] and throw me down?
I'm like a leaning wall, *just* a tottering fence *to them.*
⁴ Certainly they plan to throw me down from my high position.   Selah
They love lies—bless with their mouths, but curse in their hearts.

⁵ O my soul, wait in silence for God alone;
   For my hope comes from him.
⁶ He alone is my rock and my salvation, my defense;
I will not be shaken.
⁷ My salvation and my glory come from[b] God, my mighty rock;
My refuge is in God.

⁸ O my people,
   Trust in him at all times;
   Pour out your hearts to him.
   God is our refuge.   Selah
      ⁹ Mankind[c] is only a breath—the sons of man delude themselves.[d]
      Placed upon scales, they are altogether lighter than a breath.[e]

¹⁰ Do not trust in oppression or hold false hopes about robbery.
If your riches increase, don't set your heart upon them.
   ¹¹ One *thing* God has spoken, which I have heard twice:[f] "Power *belongs* to God."
   ¹² And lovingkindness, O Lord, is yours *also,*
      Surely you repay everyone according to what he has done.

---

a   Literally, "this man."

b   Literally, "rest on."

c   Literally, "the sons of man." This term, meaning mankind, occurs twice in this verse. Many scholars,
    seeing a similar passage in Ps. 49:1-2, believe this is a comment about the common futility of poor
    people ("poor people are a breath") and rich people ("rich people delude themselves").

d   Literally, "are a lie."

e   Or "than vanity."

f   Or, "two things I have heard."

69

Psalm 63
Thirsting for God

A psalm of David. *About* when he was in the wilderness of Judah.

1 O God, you are my God.
   I am seeking you earnestly;
   My soul thirsts for you;
   My flesh longs for you in this dry weary waterless land;
2 I have seen you in the sanctuary, seen your power and your glory.

3 Because your lovingkindness is better than life:
   My lips will praise you;
   4 I will bless you as long as I live;
   I will lift up my hands *to praise* your name;[a]
   5 My mouth will sing praises with joyful lips—satisfying my soul like rich fat food;[b]
   6 I will think of you when I'm on my bed and meditate upon you during the night watches;
   7 I will sing joyfully in the shadow of your wings, because you are my help;
   8 My soul clings to you—your right hand holds me up.

9 Those who seek to destroy my life shall
   Go down to the depths of the earth;
   10 Be delivered over to the power of the sword; and
   Become food[c] for jackals.
11 And the king will rejoice in God.
   Everyone who swears by God's name[d] will celebrate,
   And the mouths of liars will be stopped.

Psalm 64
Praying and Trusting for Protection

A psalm of David.
To the music director.

1 O God, hear my voice, my complaint:
   Guard my life from my fear of the enemy;
   2 Hide me
      From the conspiracy of the wicked;
      From the throng who do evil;

---

a Literally, "my hands in your name."
b Literally, "like marrow and fatness."
c Literally, "a portion."
d Literally, "by him."

³ From those
  Who sharpen their tongues like swords,
  Who aim their bitter words like arrows ⁴ to shoot the innocent in secret
      (Suddenly they are shooting them without fear!);
  ⁵ Who encourage*ᵃ* each other in evil matters;
  Who talk about hiding snares; saying, "Who will notice?"
  ⁶ Who look *for opportunities* for injustice;
      Saying, "We have devised*ᵇ* a well-conceived plot."
          (The innermost thoughts and the heart of man are deep.)

⁷ God will shoot the wicked*ᶜ* with an arrow;
Suddenly they will be wounded;
⁸ He will make them stumble, *even* turn their tongues against themselves.
All who see them will wag their heads;
⁹ And all mankind will fear, will speak about the works of God and consider what
he has done.

¹⁰ Let the righteous rejoice in the LORD and trust in him;
Let all the upright in heart glory *in the Lord.*

Psalm 65
Praise to God

A psalm and song of David.
To the music director.

¹ O God,
    Praise waits for you in Zion;
    Vows to you will be fulfilled.
² O you who hear prayer,
    All mankind*ᵈ* must*ᵉ* come to you.
  ³ Though the record of our sins overwhelms us, you forgive our transgressions!
  ⁴ Blessed are those you choose to draw near you, to dwell in your courts.
  May we be satisfied in the goodness of your house, the holiness of your
  temple.

God's Care of the Earth

⁵ You will answer us by awesome deeds of righteousness,
O God
  Our Savior,
  The hope of all *living* to the ends of earth and *beyond* the farthest seas;

---

a   Literally, "hold fast to."
b   Literally, "finished."
c   Literally, "them."
d   Literally, "flesh."
e   Or "will."

⁶ Who, armed*a* with power, formed the mountains by his strength;

⁷ Who quiets the roar of the seas, the roar of the waves and the tumult of the nations:

⁸ Those who dwell at the ends of the earth are in awe of your signs.
    You make the dawn*b* and the dusk shout for joy;

⁹ You visit and water the earth, enriching it abundantly—the streams of God are full of water;
        You provide grain, having ordained*c* it *to be that way*;

¹⁰ You water the furrows, settle down their ridges, soften them with rain and bless their growth;

¹¹ You crown the year with your bounty,
    Your pathways overflow with abundance.

¹² The grasslands of the wilderness overflow;
    The hillsides are clothed with rejoicing;

¹³ The meadows are clothed with flocks;
    The valleys also are covered over with grain;
    They shout for joy and sing.

Psalm 66
Praise for God's Mighty Works

A psalm and a song.
To the music director.

¹ Shout joyfully to God, all the earth;

² Sing out the glory of his name;
    Make his praise glorious.

³ Say to God,
    "How awesome are your works!
    Your power is so great that your enemies cringe before you.

⁴ All the earth will worship you, will sing to you—sing your name."   Selah

⁵ Come and see what God has done,*d* his awesome deeds on behalf of the children of men.

⁶ He turned the sea into dry land;
    Then they passed through the *Jordan* River on their feet—rejoice in him!

⁷ He rules by his power forever;
    His eyes keep watch on the nations—the rebellious better not*e* exalt themselves!
        Selah

---

a Literally, "girded."
b Literally, "outgoing of the morning."
c Literally, "prepared."
d Literally, "see the works of the God."
e Literally, "let not the rebellious."

⁸ Bless our God, you people.
Let the sound of his praises ring
⁹ *For him* who preserves our souls, our lives,
For him who keeps our feet from slipping.

¹⁰ For you, O God, have tested us
By refining us as silver is refined;
¹¹ By bringing us into the *enemy's* net;
By laying an oppressive burden upon our backs; and
¹² By letting men ride over our heads.
We've been through*ᵃ* fire and water,
And you have brought us out to a place of abundance.

¹³ *Now* I will go to your house with burnt offerings:
I will fulfill my vows to you
¹⁴ Which my lips uttered and my mouth spoke when I was in trouble.
¹⁵ I will offer to you burnt offerings of fat beasts and the offerings of rams;
I will offer bulls and goats.   Selah

¹⁶ Come and hear, all you who fear God,
And I will tell you what he has done for my soul.
¹⁷ For I cried out to him with my mouth and praised him with my tongue.
¹⁸ If I had cherished iniquity in my heart, the Lord would not have listened.
¹⁹ But truly, God listened.
He heard my voice in prayer;

²⁰ Blessed be God,
Who has not rejected my prayer or taken his lovingkindness from me.

Psalm 67
A Blessing

A psalm and a song.
To the music director: with stringed instruments.

¹ May God
Be gracious to us,
Bless us, and
Make his face shine upon us.   Selah

² May your way be known upon earth;
May your salvation *be known* among all nations;
³ May the peoples praise you, O God, all people praise you;
⁴ May the nations be glad and sing for joy,
For you judge people righteously
And guide the nations upon earth;   Selah
⁵ May the peoples praise you, O God, all people praise you.

---

a Literally, "gone through."

⁶ Then

The earth will yield its harvest;
God, our God, will bless us;
⁷ God will bless us;
And all the ends of the earth will fear him.

Psalm 68
Celebrating God's Victory

A psalm and song of David.
To the music director.

¹ Let God arise;
Let his enemies be scattered;
Let those who hate him flee before him.
² As smoke is blown*a* away, let them be driven away;
As wax melts before a fire, let the wicked perish before God.
³ Let the righteous be glad—rejoice before God—rejoice and be glad.

⁴ Sing to God;
Sing praises to his name;
Lift up a *song* to him who rides upon the clouds*b*—the LORD is his name;
Rejoice before him.

⁵ God is in his holy dwelling,
Yet he is
A father to the fatherless;
A protector*c* of widows;
⁶ A God who
Places the lonely in families;*d*
And leads out the prisoners to a prosperous*e* *land*;
But *makes* the rebellious dwell in a dry land.

⁷ O God,
When you went out in front of your people,
When you marched through the wilderness,   Selah
⁸ The earth shook.
Yes, the heavens poured down *rain*
Before God, the One of Sinai;
Before God, the God of Israel.
⁹ You sent abundant rain, O God;
You refreshed your inheritance when it was parched.
¹⁰ *Then* your people dwelt in it.

---

a   Literally, "driven."
b   Or "rides through the deserts."
c   Literally, "a judge."
d   Literally, "in houses."
e   Hebrew, "kosharot." An unknown term.

O God, in your goodness you provided for the needy.

¹¹ The Lord gave the word and a great company *of people*ᵃ proclaimed:
  ¹² "The kings of armies are fleeing; they are fleeing!"
The women at home divide the spoil.
  ¹³ If you lay down among the campfiresᵇ...
    The wings of the dove are covered with silver, its wings glistening of gold!
  ¹⁴ When the Almighty scattered kings, *it was like* a snowstorm on Mt. Zalmon.ᶜ

¹⁵ O mountain of God, Mt. Bashan;ᵈ
O mountain with many peaks, Mt. Bashan;
¹⁶ O many-peaked mountain:
  Why do you look with envy at *Mt. Zion,* at the mountain which God desired for his dwelling place?
  Yes, *that is* where the Lord will dwell forever.
    ¹⁷ The God who
      Has unnumbered thousandsᵉ of chariots;
      Came from Mt. Sinai to his sanctuary;
        ¹⁸ Ascended on high;ᶠ
      Took prisoners captive; and
      Received gifts from men, *even* from rebellious people.
    The Lord God dwells there.

¹⁹ Blessed be the Lord who
  Bears our burdens every day;
  Is God our savior;   Selah
    ²⁰ Is the God who delivers us;
  Is our Lord, the God who provides escapeᵍ from death;
    ²¹ Strikes the heads of his enemies, the hairy top of the head of those who *continue* walking in their sin.

²² The Lord has said,
  "I will bring *my enemies* from Bashan;
  I will bring them back from the depths of the sea
    ²³ That your feet may stompʰ in their blood,
      That the tongues of your dogs *may lick* your enemies.

²⁴ They have seen your procession, O God,
  The procession of my God and King into his sanctuary.
    ²⁵ Singers first, then musicians in the midst of maidens beating tambourines.

---

a Or "of women."
b Or "the saddlebags," or "sheep pens." The Hebrew is not clear. The sentence seems incomplete.
c Literally, "it snowed on Mt. Zalmon." "Mt. Zalmon": an unidentified height, perhaps in Samaria near Mt. Gerizim. Snow is rare in this area.
d Probably a reference to Mr. Hermon, which is on the northern border of Bashan.
e Literally, "the chariots of God are myriads, thousands upon thousands."
f Literally, "you have ascended." The translation reflects Ephesians 4:8.
g Literally, "to whom belong escapes."
h Literally, "shatter."

²⁶ Bless God, you congregation *of Israel;*
  Bless the L<small>ORD</small>, you fountain of Israel.
    ²⁷ *Look,* there's
        The tribe of Benjamin, the least of them, leading;
        The princes of Judah in their raiment;^{*a*}
        The princes of Zebulun and
        The princes of Naphtali.

²⁸ Summon your power, O God;
      The strength, O God, by which you worked *wonders* for us;
    ²⁹ Then kings will bring presents to you because of your temple in Jerusalem.
³⁰ Rebuke
      The beasts *living* in the reeds,
      The herd of the bulls among the calves, *among* the peoples;
  Trample underfoot their pieces of silver;
  Scatter the people who delight in war;
    ³¹ Then envoys will come from Egypt, and
      Cush will soon stretch out her hands to God.

³² You kingdoms of the earth:
      Sing to God;
      Sing praises to the Lord,   Selah
    ³³ To him
        Who rides upon the highest heavens;^{*b*}
        Who sends out his voice, his mighty voice.
    ³⁴ Ascribe^{*c*} power to God,
        Whose majesty is over Israel and
        Whose power is in the skies;
      Like this:
        ³⁵ "God is awesome in his sanctuary.
        The God of Israel gives strength and power to his people.
        Blessed be God."

Psalm 69
Prayer of Confession for Deliverance

A psalm of David.
To the music director: *to the tune of* "The Lilies."

  ¹ Save me, O God,
      For the waters are rising^{*d*} to my neck;
    ² I am sinking in a deep mire where there is no foothold;

---

a Or "throngs of princes of Judah."

b Or "ancient heavens."

c "Ascribe": credit a person with having.

d Literally, "have come to."

I have come into deep waters—the flood engulfs me;
³ I am weary of crying *for help;*
My throat is parched;
My eyes fail while I wait for my God.
⁴ Those who hate me without reason number more*ᵃ* than the hairs of my head.
My enemies, who would destroy me with lies,*ᵇ* are so mighty that I *am forced
to* restore what I did not steal!

⁵ O God,
You know my follies;
The wrongs I have done are not hidden from you.
⁶ O Lord God of hosts,
Do not let those who hope in you be ashamed because of me.
O God of Israel,
Do not let those who seek you be dishonored because of me.

⁷ I have borne reproach for your sake;
Humiliation has covered my face;
⁸ I have become a stranger to my brothers, an alien to my mother's sons.
⁹ Zeal for your house consumes me;
The insults of those who scorn you have fallen upon me.
¹⁰ When I weep and fast, they mock me;
¹¹ When I make sackcloth my clothing, I become an object of their ridicule.
¹² Those who sit at the city gate talk *against me,* and
I am the song of drunkards.

¹³ But as for me,
My prayer is to you, O LORD.
Hear me
At an acceptable time, O God;
In the abundance of your lovingkindness;
With your saving faithfulness.
¹⁴ Deliver me from this mire—don't let me sink;
Deliver me from those who hate me—out of the deep *waters.*
¹⁵ Do not let the floodwaters drown me,*ᶜ* the deep waters swallow me, or the
pit shut her mouth over me.
¹⁶ Answer me, O LORD,
For your lovingkindness is good;
Turn to me according to your great compassion;
¹⁷ Do not hide your face from your servant,
For I am in trouble;
Answer me quickly—¹⁸ draw near to my soul—redeem me—ransom me from
my foes.

---

a Literally, "are more."
b Or "without cause."
c Literally, "overflow me."

19 You know how they mock, scorn and dishonor me—all my foes are before you;

20 *Their* reproaches have broken my heart—*to the point* of despair;
When I looked for sympathy, there was none—I found no comforters.

21 They put poison in my meat,
And for my thirst they gave me vinegar.

22 Let their *bountiful* table before them become a snare;
When they are at peace, let *their allies become*[a] a snare.

23 Let their eyes be darkened so they cannot see, and
Make their loins shake continually.

24 Pour your indignation on them, and
Let your fierce anger grip them.

25 Let their camps be deserted, and
Let no one dwell in their tents;

26 Because they persecute the one whom you yourself have smitten;
And they gossip[b] about the pain of those whom you have wounded.

27 Pile up their sins;[c]
Do not let them enter into your righteousness;

28 Let them be blotted out of the Book of Life,[d] not be recorded as among the righteous.

29 I am afflicted[e] and in pain.
Let your salvation, O God, put me out of their reach.[f]

30 I will sing praises to God's name;
I will magnify him with thanksgiving.

31 This will please the LORD more than *sacrificing* an ox or bull with horns and hoofs.

32 The humble will see it and be glad.

You who seek God, let your hearts revive;

33 For the LORD hears the needy.
He does not despise his *own people who are* prisoners.[g]

34 Let heaven and earth and the seas and everything that moves in them praise him;

35 For God will save Zion and build up[h] the cities of Judah,
That his people[i] may dwell there and possess it.

36 The descendants of his servants will inherit it,
And those who love his name will dwell in it.

---

a Literally, "let it become a snare."
b Literally, "talk."
c Literally, "set their sin upon their sin."
d Or "record," or "book of the living"
e Or "lowly."
f Literally, "set me inaccessibly high."
g Literally, "does not despise his."
h Or "rebuild."
i Literally, "they."

Psalm 70
A Cry for Speedy Deliverance

A psalm of David
To the music director: to call to mind.

1 O God, rescue me;
O Lord, hurry and help me.
2 Let those
Who seek my life be humiliated and ashamed;
Who delight in my pain be turned back in disgrace;
3 Who *contemptuously* say, "Aha! Aha!" be turned back because of their
shameful behavior.[a]
4 Let all those who seek you rejoice and be glad in you;
Let those who love your salvation say continually, "God is great."[b]

5 But I am poor and needy;
O God, my help and my deliverer, hurry to me.
O Lord, do not delay.

Psalm 71
Taking Refuge in God

1 O Lord, I take refuge in you.
Let me never be put to shame;
2 Rescue me and deliver me in your righteousness;
Listen to me[c] and save me;
3 Be my rock of refuge to which I may always go.
Give the command to save me,
For you are my rock and my fortress.

4 Deliver me, O my God
From the grasp[d] of the wicked,
From the grasp of unjust and cruel men.
5 For you are my hope, O Lord GOD;
You are my confidence from my youth.
6 I have been sustained by you since birth;[e]
You are the one[f] who took me out of my mother's womb.
My praise is continually of you.

7 I am *seen* as a wonder by many, but you are my strong refuge.

---

a Literally, "because of their shame."
b Or "let God be magnified."
c Literally, "incline your ear."
d Literally, "from the hand." And next line.
e Literally, "from the womb."
f Literally, "he."

⁸ My mouth is filled with your praise and *declares* your glory all day long.

⁹ Do not cast me off when I am old;*ᵃ*
  Do not forsake me when my strength fails;
    ¹⁰ For my enemies speak against me;
      Those who are waiting to kill me*ᵇ* are plotting together,
    ¹¹ Saying,
        "God has forsaken him;
        Let's pursue and seize him;
            For there is no one to rescue him."
¹² O God,
        Do not be far away;
  O my God,
      Quickly, help me.
        ¹³ Let my life's opponents*ᶜ* be put to shame, *even* consumed;
          Let those who seek to hurt me be covered with scorn and disgrace.

¹⁴ I will hope *in you* continually, praise you even more and more.
¹⁵ My mouth will speak of your *acts of* righteousness and salvation all day long,
      Even though I don't know their number.*ᵈ*
¹⁶ I will go in your strength, Lord GOD;
  I will remind them of your righteousness, yours alone.

---

      ¹⁷ O God,
          You have taught me from my youth,
          And ever since I have declared your wondrous works.
        ¹⁸ When I am old and gray, O God, do not forsake me until
        I have shown
            Your strength to this generation and
            Your power to all generations to come.
      ¹⁹ God,
          Your righteousness *reaches* to the heavens;
          You have done great things—who, O God, is like you?
        ²⁰ You who have shown me many troubles and distresses
            Will revive me;
            Will bring me up again from the depths of the earth;
          ²¹ Will increase my greatness; and
            Will comfort me again.

---

²² I will also praise you with the harp for your faithfulness, O my God;
  I will sing praises to you with the lyre, O Holy One of Israel;

---

a   Literally, "in time of old age."
b   Literally, "watch for my life."
c   Or "adversaries of my soul."
d   The Hebrew is not clear.

²³ My lips will shout for joy when I sing praises to you;
And my soul *will sing,*
> For you have redeemed me.
²⁴ My tongue also will talk of your righteous deeds all day long,
> For those who sought to hurt me will be humiliated and put to shame.

Psalm 72
Prayer for a King

A psalm of Solomon

¹ God,

> Give your *love of* justice to the king;
> And *give* your righteousness to the king's son;
> ² *So that* he
> > Will judge your people with righteousness and your poor^{*a*} with justice
> > (³ So the mountains and the hills will yield peace to the people
> > > *As a result* of righteousness);
> > ⁴ Will defend the poor among the people;
> > Will save the children of the needy; and
> > Will crush the oppressor;
> > > (⁵ So they will fear you as long as the sun and moon endure, throughout all generations.)

⁶ May the king be like rain falling upon a sheared field, like showers watering the earth;
⁷ May the righteous flourish in his days;
May peace abound until the moon is no more;
⁸ May he reign from sea to sea, from the River *Euphrates* to the ends of the earth.
> ⁹ Let the desert tribes bow before him and his enemies lick the dust;
> ¹⁰ Let the kings of Tarshish and the coastland *nations* bring tribute;
> Let the kings of Sheba and Seba bring gifts;
> ¹¹ Let all kings fall down before him, all nations serve him.
¹² For he will
> Deliver the needy, the poor who have no one to help them, when they cry out;
> ¹³ Have pity on the poor^{*b*} and save the lives of the needy
> > ¹⁴ By redeeming their lives from deceit and violence,
> > For to him^{*c*} their blood is precious.

¹⁵ May he live *a long time;*
May the gold of Sheba be given to him;

---

a Or "afflicted."
b Or "weak."
c Literally, "in his sight."

May *people* pray for blessings upon him[a] all day long;

16 May there be an abundance of grain on the earth—even to the tops of the mountains.

Let the heads of grain[b] wave like *the cedars of* Lebanon;
Let the cities flourish like grass of the earth.

17 May his name endure for ever;
May his name continue as long as the sun *shines*;
May people be blessed through him; and
May all nations call him blessed.

Closing Doxology

18 Blessed be the LORD God, the God of Israel
Who alone does wondrous things.

19 Blessed be his glorious name for ever;
May the whole earth be filled with his glory;
Amen and Amen.

20 The prayers of David, the son of Jesse, are ended.

BOOK THREE

Psalm 73

A psalm of Asaph.

Prosperity of the Wicked Bemoaned

1 Truly God is good to Israel, to those who are pure in heart.

2 But as for me, my feet almost slipped, my steps almost strayed;

3 For I was envious of the proud[c] when I saw the prosperity of the wicked.

4 For they

Do not have *life's* pangs before they die, their bodies are fat;

5 Do not have the troubles of other men; and
Are not stricken like other people.

6 Therefore:

Pride is their necklace;
A garment of wrong *deeds*[d] covers them;

7 Their eyes bulge, *wanting* the finest;[e]
The imaginations of their heart run wild;

8 They scoff and speak loftily and wickedly about oppressing *others*;

9 They set their mouth against the heavens while their tongues parade throughout the earth.

---

a   Or "pray for him and bless him."

b   Literally, "its fruit."

c   Or "arrogant."

d   Or "of violence."

e   Or "eyes bulge with fatness."

¹⁰ Therefore the people return to them and drink their waters of abundance,

¹¹ Saying,

> "How will God know?"
>
> "Is the Most High aware?"*ᵃ*

¹² Look at the wicked—always at ease and increasing their wealth.

¹³ Surely I have kept my heart pure, kept my hands clean and innocent*ᵇ* for nothing.

¹⁴ For all the day long they plague me, rebuking me *every* morning.

Prosperity of the Wicked Understood

¹⁵ I would have been a traitor to this generation of your people if I had spoken about what *I was thinking (i.e., verses 4-5 above).*

¹⁶ When I tried*ᶜ* to understand this, it troubled me;*ᵈ*

¹⁷ Until I went into the sanctuary of God—then I understood their destiny.

> ¹⁸ Surely, you have put them on slippery *ground;*
>
> You will cast them down to destruction.
>
> ¹⁹ How they will be brought to ruin—in a moment—in complete terror!
>
> ²⁰ After you rise *against them,* O Lord, you will despise the *mind's* image of them as when one wakes up from a *bad* dream.

Asaph Repents

²¹ When my heart was bitter and I was pricked deep within,*ᵉ*

> ²² I was senseless, ignorant like an *unthinking* animal before you.

²³ Nevertheless,

> I am continually with you;
>
> You hold my right hand;
>
> ²⁴ You guide me with your counsel;
>
> And after this you will receive me into glory.

²⁵ Who else do I have in heaven?

And beside you, who else would I desire upon earth?

> ²⁶ Though my flesh and my heart fade away, God is my heart's rock and my portion forever.

²⁷ For surely

> Those who are far from you will perish;
>
> You destroy all those who are unfaithful to you.

²⁸ But as for me, it is good to be near to God.

I have made the LORD God my refuge,

> That I may tell about all your works.

---

a   Literally, "is there knowledge with the most high."

b   Literally, "washed my hands in innocence."

c   Literally, "when I thought."

d   Literally, "was troubling in my sight."

e   Literally, "pricked in the kidney," the part of the body which they envisioned as the repository of one's moral character, of one's secret thoughts and feelings.

Psalm 74
Why Has God Deserted Us?

A maskil of Asaph.

¹ O God,
  Why have you cast us off forever?
  Why does your anger smolder against the sheep of your pasture?
  ² Remember
    Your congregation—which you purchased long ago;
    The tribe of your inheritance—which you have redeemed; *and*
    Mt. Zion—where you have dwelt.
  ³ Turn your footsteps toward these everlasting ruins,
    For the enemy has damaged everything in the sanctuary.
      ⁴ Your enemies have roared in the midst of the place where you meet us.
  ⁷ᵇ *Look*, they have defiled the dwelling place of your name *by*:
    Setting up their banners as signs;
      ⁵⁻⁶ Smashing all the carved *panels and pillars* with axes and hammers*ᵃ*
        Like men hacking*ᵇ* with axes in a thicket of trees; and
      ⁷ᵃ Burning your sanctuary to the ground.
  ⁸ They have said in their hearts, "Let's completely subdue them."
    They have burned up all the meeting places of God in the land.
  ⁹ We don't see any *miraculous* signs or prophets anymore;
    Not one among us knows how long *it will continue.*

¹⁰ O God,
  How long will the enemy mock *you*?
  Will this enemy revile your name forever?
    ¹¹ Why do you hold back your hand, your right hand *of power.*
    Take it out of the folds of your garment*ᶜ* and destroy them.

¹² You, O God, are my king of old;
  Your work rescues on the earth.*ᵈ*
    ¹³ You divided the sea by your strength;
      You broke the heads of the monsters in the waters;
    ¹⁴ You crushed the heads of Leviathan*ᵉ* and gave him to the desert folk*ᶠ* for food;
    ¹⁵ You broke open springs and streams;
      You dried up ever-flowing rivers.

¹⁶ The day is yours;
  The night is also yours;

---

a   Or "and picks," or "and hatchets."
b   Literally, "lifting above."
c   Literally, "your bosom."
d   Literally, "in the midst of the earth."
e   Probably a reference to the many-headed mythological creature, not the Leviathan of Job 41:1.
f   Or "creatures."

You established the sun and *other* luminaries;
¹⁷ You set all the boundaries of the earth; and
You made summer and winter.

¹⁸ O Lord,
Remember how the enemy mocked you—that these foolish people have
reviled^a your name!
¹⁹ Do not give the life^b of your dove to the wild beast;
Do not forget the lives of your afflicted forever;
²⁰ Have respect for the covenant, for the dark places of the land are full of places
where violence dwells.^c
²¹ Do not let the downtrodden retreat ashamed;
Let the poor and needy praise your name.

²² Rise up, O God;
Defend your cause;
Remember how the foolish man scoffs at you all day long;
²³ Do not forget the voice of your enemies, the uproar of those that rise up
against you increases continually.

Psalm 75
God Is the Judge

A psalm and song of Asaph.
To the music director, *to the tune of* "Do Not Destroy."

¹ We give thanks to you, O God;
We give thanks to you for being near.^d
People^e tell of your wondrous works.

² *God has said,*
"When I select the appointed time, I will judge with equity.
³ When the earth and all its inhabitants quake, I hold up its pillars."   Selah

⁴ *So* I say to the arrogant, "Do not boast;"
And to the wicked,
"Do not lift up your horn;
⁵ Do not lift up your horns on high;^f
Do not speak with an arrogant attitude."^g

---

a "Revile": attack verbally, often with abusive language.
b Or "deliver the soul."
c Literally, "of habitations of violence."
d Literally, "for your name is near."
e Literally, "they."
f "Lift up your horns on high." Picture a wild ox lifting its head of horns as a challenge.
g Literally, "arrogant neck."

⁶ For no one from the east or the west or from the desert can promote^a a man,
   ⁷ For God is the judge—he lifts up one and brings down another.
      ⁸ For in the hand of the LORD there is a cup of foaming wine mixed *with spices*—and he pours it out—and all the wicked of the earth shall drink it down to the dregs.

⁹ I will declare this forever—singing praises to the God of Jacob.
¹⁰ He will cut off all the horns of the wicked,
   But the horns of the righteous will be lifted up.

Psalm 76
God, the Powerful Judge

A psalm and song of Asaph.
To the music director: with stringed instruments.

   ¹ God is known in Judah; his name is great in Israel.
   ² His tabernacle^b is in Salem; his dwelling place is in Zion;
      ³ For there he broke the arrows, shields and swords—the weapons of war *of our enemies.*   Selah

⁶ᵃ O God of Jacob,^c
      ⁴ You are more glorious and majestic than mountains *rich* with game;
         ⁵ For our stouthearted *enemies lie* plundered.
            They've slept their *last* sleep;
            None of those men of war can use their hands anymore; and
      ⁶ᵇ Due to your rebuke, both their horses and riders lay still.
   ⁷ You truly^d are to be feared.
         Who can stand before you when you are angry?
      ⁸ You have caused *your* judgment to be heard from heaven;
         The earth feared and was still ⁹ when God arose
            To *establish* judgment and save all the meek of the earth.   Selah
         ¹⁰ Surely your wrath against *wicked* man will bring you praise;
            And you will restrain the survivors of your wrath.^e

¹¹ Make vows and fulfill *them* to the LORD your God.
   Let all who are around him bring gifts to him
      Who ought to be feared,
   ¹² Who cuts off the *haughty* spirit of princes, and
      Who is feared by the kings of the earth.

---

a   Literally, "lift up."
b   "Tabernacle": a place where God dwells and is worshipped. Or "abode."
c   "O God of Jacob" has been moved up from 76:6.
d   Literally, "you you" [sic].
e   The Hebrew of this verse is not clear.

86

Psalm 77
Seeking God in the Day of Trouble

A psalm of Asaph.
For Jeduthun, the music director."

¹ I cry to God with my voice, to God with my voice; and he hears.
² I seek the Lord in the day of my trouble;
  My hand stretches out *all* night without tiring;
    And my soul refuses to be comforted.
³ I remember God, and moan;
  I sigh, and my spirit grows faint.   Selah
⁴ You keep me awake;*a*
  I am so troubled that I cannot speak.

⁵ I think about days of old, years of old;
⁶ I remember my songs in the night;
  I meditate with my heart;
  And my spirit wonders:
    ⁷ Will the Lord reject me forever?
      Will he show favor no more?
    ⁸ Is his lovingkindness gone forever?
      Have his promises ceased forever?
    ⁹ Has God forgotten to be gracious?
      Has he withheld his compassion in anger?   Selah
¹⁰ And I declare,
      "This may be what I grieve about*b today,
      But I *remember* the years of the right hand of the Most High;
        ¹¹ I remember the works of the LORD;
          Yes, I remember his wonders of old."

  And I say to the Lord,
    ¹² "I will meditate on all your works, and
      I will talk about your deeds.

    "Your ways, O God, are holy.
  ¹³ What god is as great as our God?
  ¹⁴ You are the God who works wonders;
    You have displayed your power among the peoples;
  ¹⁵ You have redeemed your people, the descendants of Jacob and Joseph,
      With your mighty arm.   Selah

  ¹⁶ "The waters saw you, O God, the waters saw you and trembled;
    The depths also quaked;
  ¹⁷ The clouds poured down rain;
    The skies thundered;

---

a Literally, "hold the guards of my eyes."
b Or "this is my grief." The Hebrew is not clear.

Your lightning bolts*a* flashed;
18 The sound of your thunder was in the whirlwind;*b*
Your lightning lit up the world; and
The earth trembled and shook.

19 "Your path went through the Red Sea.
Though your footprints were unseen,*c* your path was in the great waters.
20 You led your people like a flock by the hand of Moses and Aaron."

Psalm 78
God's Faithfulness to Israel

A maskil of Asaph.

1 Listen, O my people, to my teaching;
Incline your ears to the words of my mouth.
2 I will open my mouth in a parable;
I will utter mysteries of old
3 That we have heard and have known,
That our fathers have told us.

4 We will not hide them from our children;
We will tell the next generation about
The praiseworthy deeds*d* of the LORD,
His strength, and
The wonderful deeds that he has done.
5 *We will tell*
How he:
Decreed statutes*e* to Jacob;
Established a law for Israel; and
Ordered our fathers to teach them to their children
6 That the next generation would know them;
Even the children yet to be born,
Who should *then* arise and tell their children;
7 That they would:
Set their hope in God;
Not forget the works of God;
Keep his commandments; and
8 Not be as their fathers, who were:
A stubborn and rebellious generation,

---

a Literally, "arrows."
b "Whirlwind": a column of air rapidly rotating around a low pressure core. A metaphor for a terrible destructive force or a rapid succession of destructive events.
c Literally, "not known."
d Literally, "praises."
e Literally, "established a testimony."

A generation that did not prepare its heart *for God,*
A generation whose spirit was not faithful to God.
(⁹ *For example,* the children of Ephraim
Turned back in the day of battle
Though they were armed, carrying bows;
¹⁰ Did not keep the covenant of God;
Refused to walk in his law; ¹¹ and
Forgot the works and wonders he had shown them.)

How he:
¹² Did miracles in the sight of their fathers in the land of Egypt,
In the fields of Zoan;
¹³ Divided the sea, made the water stand up like a wall and led them through;
¹⁴ Led them with a cloud in the daytime and a light of fire all night;
¹⁵ Split the rocks in the wilderness,
Giving *water* abundantly, as from the deep;
¹⁶ Brought out of the rock streams of water that ran like rivers.

¹⁷ *How* Israel:[a]
Continued to sin against him;
Rebelled against the most High in the wilderness;
¹⁸ Tested God in their heart by demanding the food they craved; and
¹⁹ Spoke against God, saying:
"Can God spread a table in the wilderness?
²⁰ Sure, he struck the rock so that the waters gushed out and the streams
overflowed, but
Can he give us bread?
Will he provide food for his people?"

²¹ *How* when the Lᴏʀᴅ heard them, he was full of wrath; his fire was kindled
against Jacob and his anger against Israel;
²² Because they did not believe in God or trust in his deliverance[b] ²³ though he
had:
Commanded the clouds above and opened the doors of heaven;
²⁴ Rained manna upon them to eat;
Given them grain from heaven—²⁵ man ate angels' food!
Sent them food in abundance;
²⁶ Caused an east wind to blow in the heavens and by his power brought in
the south wind; and
²⁷ Rained food upon them like dust, winged birds like the sand of the
seashore, ²⁸ and let it fall all around their dwellings in the midst of their
camp.

²⁹ *How* they ate and were full because he had given them what they desired.
³⁰ *How* before they satisfied their desire, while their food was *still* in their mouths,

---

a Literally, "they."
b Or "saving power."

³¹ The wrath of God came upon them

    And slew *some of* the strongest of them,

    And struck down *some of* the best men of Israel.

³² *We will tell how:*

  Despite all this

    They still sinned;

    They did not believe in his wondrous works; ³³ and

    They finished their days in futility and years in fear.*ᵃ*

³⁴ When he killed *some of* them, then:

    They would seek him;

    They would return and diligently seek God.

  ³⁵ They remembered that God was

      Their Rock,

      The Most High God, and

      Their Redeemer.

  ³⁶ Nevertheless, they

      Flattered him with their mouth and

      Lied to him with their tongues;

      ³⁷ For their hearts were not steadfast toward him,

        And they were not faithful to his covenant.

³⁸ *How* he, being compassionate:

      Atoned for their iniquity;

      Did not destroy them;

      Oftentimes restrained his anger;

      And did not arouse all of his wrath.

      ³⁹ For he remembered that they were but flesh, a wind that passes and does not return.

⁴⁰ *How:*

    Often they rebelled against him in the wilderness and grieved him in the desert!

  ⁴¹ Again and again they tempted God and pained the Holy One of Israel.

  ⁴² They did not remember

    His power;

    The day when he redeemed them from the enemy; or

    ⁴³ *How* he had:

      Done his miracles in Egypt and his wonders in the fields of Zoan;

      ⁴⁴ Turned rivers and streams into blood so the Egyptians*ᵇ* couldn't drink;

      ⁴⁵ Sent swarms of flies that devoured them and frogs that destroyed;

      ⁴⁶ Given their crops to grasshoppers and the product *of their labor* to locusts;

      ⁴⁷ Destroyed their vines with hail and their sycamore trees with frost;

---

a   Literally, "terror."

b   Literally, "they."

⁴⁸ Given their cattle to the hail and their herds to thunderbolts;
⁴⁹ Loosed upon them his burning anger, wrath and indignation
>> *By sending* trouble, a band of destroying angels.
>>> (⁵⁰ He prepared a path for his anger.
>>>> He did not spare their lives from death,
>>>> But gave their lives over to plagues.)
⁵¹ Struck down all the firstborn in Egypt—the firstfruits of the virility of the tents of Ham;

⁵² *How* he:
>> Led his people *out of Egypt* like sheep;
>> Guided them in the wilderness like a flock;
>> ⁵³ Led them safely so they were not afraid, and
>> *Made* the sea engulf their enemies;
>> ⁵⁴ Brought them to the border of his holy *land,*
>>> The hill country that his right hand had taken *for them;*
>> ⁵⁵ Drove out the *heathen* nations before them;
>> Allocated^a to them *land,* an inheritable possession; and
>> Settled the tribes of Israel in their tents.
⁵⁶ *How* they:
>> Tested and rebelled against the Most High God;
>> Did not obey what he said;^b
>> ⁵⁷ Turned away;
>> Acted unfaithfully^c like their fathers;
>> Turned aside like an unreliable bow;
>> ⁵⁸ Provoked him to anger with their high places;^dand
>> Aroused his jealousy with their idols.

We will tell
⁵⁹ *How,* when God heard this, he:
> Was filled *with wrath;*
> Vehemently rejected Israel;
> ⁶⁰ Abandoned his dwelling at Shiloh—*abandoned* the tent he had set up^e among men!
> ⁶¹ Delivered his strength, *Israel,* into captivity—*delivered* his glory, *Israel,* into the hand of his enemy!
> ⁶² Gave his people over to the sword; and
> Was furious with his inheritance.

How:
⁶³ Their young men were devoured by fire;

---

a Literally, "apportioned and measured."
b Literally, "did not obey his testimonies"; or "did not obey his laws."
c Or "treacherously."
d "High places": hills upon which idols were worshipped.
e Or "where he dwelt."

Their maidens were not given in marriage;[a]

⁶⁴ Their priests fell by the sword; and their widows could not mourn *them*.

⁶⁵ The LORD awakened as though from sleep—calling out like a warrior *moved by* wine and:

⁶⁶ Drove his enemies back, putting them to eternal shame.

⁶⁷ Rejected the tents of Joseph *and* did not choose the tribe of Ephraim;

⁶⁸ Chose the tribe of Judah, and Mt. Zion, which he loved;

⁶⁹ Built his sanctuary like the heights;
Like the earth he established forever.

⁷⁰ Chose David as his servant, taking him from the sheep pens;

⁷¹ From tending the sheep he brought him to shepherd his people, Jacob, his inheritance Israel.

⁷² *How David* shepherded them with integrity of heart and led them with skillful hands.

Psalm 79
Prayer of the Crushed

A psalm of Asaph.

¹ O God, the *heathen* nations have:
Invaded your inheritance;
Defiled your holy temple;
Laid Jerusalem in ruins;

² *Given* your servants' dead bodies to the birds of the air[b] for food;
Given the flesh of your godly ones to the beasts of the earth; and

³ Poured out their blood like water all around Jerusalem—*such that* there is no one to bury them!

⁴ We have become a reproach to our neighbors, scorned and ridiculed by those around us.

⁵ How long, O Lord?
Will you be angry forever?
Will your jealousy burn like fire?

⁶ Pour out your wrath
Upon the *heathen* nations who do not know you, and
Upon the kingdoms that do not call upon your name;

⁷ For they have devoured Jacob, and laid waste his dwelling place.

⁸ Don't hold the sins of our forefathers against us;
Let your compassion come to us quickly;
For we are in desperate need.[c]

---

a Literally, "had no glory."

b Literally, "sky"; or "heavens."

c Literally, "brought very low."

⁹ Help us, O God of our salvation,*ᵃ* for the glory of your name;
Deliver us; and
Atone for our sins for your name's sake.

¹⁰ Why should the *heathen* nations ask, "Where is their God?"
Before our eyes make it known among those nations that you avenge the
outpoured blood of your servants.
¹¹ Let the groans of the prisoners come before you;
Preserve those condemned to die according to your great power;
¹² Return into the bosom of our neighbors sevenfold the mocking with which
they have mocked you, O Lord.
¹³ Then we, your people, the sheep of your pasture,
Will give you thanks forever;
And will tell all generations about your praiseworthiness.*ᵇ*

Psalm 80
Prayer for the Restoration of Israel

A Psalm of Asaph.
To the music director: *to the tune of* "The Lily of the Covenant."*ᶜ*

¹ Listen, O Shepherd of Israel,
You who lead Joseph's *descendants* like a flock;
You who are enthroned above the cherubim.
Shine ² before Ephraim, Benjamin and Manasseh;
Stir up your strength;
Come save us.
³ Restore us, O God, and
Let your face shine *upon us* that we may be saved.

⁴ O LORD God of hosts,
How long will you be angry with your people's prayers?
⁵ You have:
Fed us the bread of tears;
Made us drink tears in great measure;
⁶ Made us an object of scorn to our neighbors.
Our enemies laugh *at us* among themselves.
⁷ Restore us, O God of hosts;
Let your face shine *upon us,* that we may be saved.

⁸ You:
Brought a vine out of Egypt;
Cast out the *heathen* nations and planted *Israel;* and

---

a   Or "rescuing God," or "saving God."
b   Literally, "will give to all generations forever your praise."
c   Or "Lily of the Testimony."

⁹ Cleared the ground before us.
We took root and filled the land.
　¹⁰ The hills were covered with our shadow, and
　　Our boughs*a* were like the mighty cedars.
　¹¹ We spread our boughs to the sea, our branches to the river.
¹² So why have you broken down our hedges?
　　All who pass by the way pluck us;
　　¹³ The boars from the woods ravage us; and
　　The beasts of the field devour us.

¹⁴ O God of hosts:
　　Turn now;
　　Look down from heaven and see;
　　Take care of this vine,
　　　¹⁵ The shoot your right hand has planted,
　　　The son you made strong for yourself.
　　　　¹⁶ For we are being burned with fire, cut down and perishing under the
　　　　frown*b* of your face.
¹⁷ Let your hand be
　　Upon the man at your right hand,
　　Upon the son of man whom you made strong for yourself.
　　　¹⁸ Then we will not turn back from you.
　　Revive us, and we will call upon your name;
¹⁹ Restore us again, O LORD God of hosts;
　Let your face shine *upon us*, that we may be saved.

Psalm 81
A Call to Faithfulness

A psalm of Asaph.
To the music director: *according to* gittith.*c*

　¹ Sing aloud to God, our strength;
　Shout joyfully to the God of Jacob;
　² Raise a song and strike the tambourine;
　Play the pleasant sounding harp and the lyre;
　³ Blow the ram's horn upon the new moon and full moon, on the day of our
　festival;
　　⁴ For this is a statute for Israel and a law of the God of Jacob.
　　⁵ He made it a statute through Joseph
　　　When he went throughout the land of Egypt,
　　　When we heard a language we didn't know,

---

a　"Bough": one of a tree's main branches.

b　Literally, "rebuke."

c　"Gittith": an undefined musical or liturgical term, or a tune or a musical instrument.

God has said:
6 "I removed the burden from *Israel's* shoulder *in Egypt;*
I set your hands free from *carrying* baskets;
7 I delivered you when you called in your trouble;
I answered you out of the dark thunder cloud;*a* and
I tested you at the waters of Meribah.   Selah

8 "O my people, listen and I will warn you;
O Israel, if *only* you would listen to me!
9 There must not be any strange god among you,
Nor may you worship any foreign god.
10 I am the LORD your God who brought you out of the land of Egypt;
Open your mouth wide, and I will fill it.

11 "But my people would not listen to my voice;
Israel would not submit to me.
12 So I gave them up
To the stubbornness of their hearts,
To walk in their own counsel.

13 "Oh, that my people would listen to me;
Oh, that Israel would walk in my ways!
14 I would quickly subdue their enemies, turn my hand against their
adversaries.
15 Those who hate the LORD would cringe before me.
Their time *of misery* would endure forever.
16 I would feed you with the finest of the wheat, and
I would satisfy you with honey out of the rock."

Psalm 82
A Call to Justice

A psalm of Asaph.

1 God presides over the congregation of *Israel's* mighty;
He judges among "the gods,"*b saying:*
2 "How long will you judge unjustly and favor the wicked?   Selah
3 Bring justice to the poor and the fatherless;
Execute it for the afflicted and needy;
4 Rescue the weak and needy;
Free them from of the hand of the wicked
5 Who know nothing,
Who do not understand, and
Who walk on in darkness.

---

a   Or "hiding place of thunder." The Hebrew is not clear.
b   "Gods": a metaphor for Israel's leaders as God's representatives on earth.

For all the foundations of the earth^a are crumbling."^{b}

⁶ I have declared *to you rulers*
   That you are gods;^{c}
   Yet all of you are children of the Most High.
      ⁷ So you will die like *all* men, fall just like any other ruler.

⁸ Rise up, O God, and judge the earth,
   For all the nations are your inheritance.

Psalm 83
Prayer for Destruction of God's Enemies

A song and psalm of Asaph.

¹ O God,
   Do not keep silent;
   Do not hold your peace;
   Do not be still, O God.
² Listen,
   Your enemies make a commotion, and
   Those who hate you are rearing their heads.
   They:
      ³ Make crafty plans against your people;
      Conspire against your treasured ones;
      ⁴ Say, "Come and let us wipe them out as a nation,
         So that the name of Israel will no longer be remembered";
      ⁵ Conspire together in one accord, covenant together against you.
         (⁶ *Those dwelling in the* tents of the Edomites, Ishmaelites, Moabites,
         Hagrites, ⁷ Gebalites, Ammonites, Amalekites, Philistines, and the
         inhabitants of Tyre. ⁸ The Assurites, who have helped the children of
         Lot, have joined them too.)   Selah
   ⁹ Do to them as you did to the Midianites; and *as you did* to Sisera and Jabin at
   the River Kison
      (¹⁰ Who perished at Endor and became dung for the earth).
   ¹¹ Make their nobles *die* like Oreb and Zeeb;
   Make all their princes *die* like Zebah and Zalmunna.
      (¹² Who said, "Let us take possession of the pastures of God.")
¹³ O my God,
   Make them
      Like whirling dust, chaff before the wind;
      ¹⁴ Like a forest fire,^{d} a flame that sets the mountains ablaze;

---

a   "Foundations of the earth": a metaphor for the justice system, civil institutions.

b   Literally, "are shaken."

c   "Gods": a metaphor for Israel's leaders as God's representatives on earth.

d   Literally, "fire that burns the forest."

¹⁵ Pursue them with your fierce storm;
Terrify them with your hurricane;
¹⁶ Fill their faces with shame until they seek your name, O Lord;
¹⁷ Let them be ashamed and dismayed forever;
Let them be humiliated and perish;
¹⁸ That they may know that you alone, whose name is Yahweh, are the most high over all the earth.

Psalm 84
Longing to be With God

A psalm of the sons of Korah.
To the music director: *according to* gittith.

¹ How lovely is your dwelling place, O Lord of hosts.
² My soul yearns, even faints, *to be in* the courts of the Lord;
My heart and my flesh cry out for*ᵃ* the living God.
   ³ Even the sparrow has found a home,
   And the swallow has a nest for herself where she may lay her young near your altars, O Lord of hosts, my King, and my God.
⁴ Blessed are those who dwell in your house ever praising you.   Selah
⁵ Blessed are those whose strength is in you,
   Whose hearts *are set on* a pilgrimage*ᵇ to Jerusalem;*
      ⁶ Who make the Valley of Weeping a place of springs when they pass through it;
         Like the autumn rain*ᶜ* that covers the valley with blessings;
      ⁷ Who go from strength to strength until every one of them appears before God in Zion.

⁸ O Lord God of hosts,
   Hear my prayer;
   Listen, O God of Jacob;   Selah
      ⁹ Look, O God our shield;
   Look upon the face of your anointed.
      ¹⁰ For a day in your courts is better than a thousand *anywhere else;*
         I would rather be a doorkeeper in the house of my God than dwell in the tents of the wicked;
            ¹¹ For the Lord God is a sun and shield;
               The Lord gives grace and glory;
               He withholds no good thing from those who walk uprightly.
¹² O Lord of hosts,
   Blessed is the man who trusts in you.

---

a   Or "sing with joy to."
b   Literally, "the pathways."
c   Literally, "early rains." The Jewish New Year occurs between September 4 and October 6..

Psalm 85
Confidence in God

To the music director.
A Psalm of the sons of Korah.

¹ Lord, you have:
  Shown favor to your land;
  Restored the fortunes of Jacob;
    ² Forgiven the iniquity of your people;
    Covered all their sin;   Selah
    ³ Set aside all of your wrath and
      Turned yourself from your burning anger.
  ⁴ O God of our salvation; *now*
    Restore us;
    Put away your indignation toward us.
      ⁵ Will you be angry with us forever?
        Will you prolong your anger to all generations?
      ⁶ Won't you revive us again so your people may rejoice in you?
  ⁷ O LORD,
    Show us your unfailing love, and
    Grant us your salvation.

⁸ I will listen to what God, YAHWEH, will say,
  For he speaks peace to his people, his godly ones;
    (*O LORD,* do not let them turn back to folly).
  ⁹ Surely his salvation is near those who fear him,
    That glory may dwell in our land.

¹⁰ Lovingkindness and faithfulness*ᵃ* have met together;
  Righteousness and peace have kissed each other;
¹¹ Faithfulness*ᵇ* springs forth from the earth;
  Righteousness looks down from heaven.
¹² Truly, the LORD will give what is good—our land will yield its harvest.
¹³ Righteousness will go before him and prepare the way for his steps.

---

a Or "and truth."
b Or "truth."

Psalm 86
Believer's Prayer for Favor

A prayer of David.

¹ O LORD,
    Incline your ear and answer me,
        For I am poor and needy;
  ² Protect my life,
        For I am a godly person;
    Save your servant who trusts in you,
        For you are my God;
  ³ Be gracious to me, O Lord,
        For I cry to you all day long;
  ⁴ Bring rejoicing to the soul of your servant,
        For I lift up my soul to you, O Lord.
⁵ For you, Lord,
  Are good;
  Ready to forgive; and
  Full of *ᵃ* lovingkindness to all who call upon you.

⁶ O LORD,
  Listen to my prayers, and
  Listen to my supplications.
  ⁷ In the day of my trouble I will call upon you,
    For you will answer me.
⁸ O Lord, among the *so called* gods
    There are none like you,
    No works *like your works.*

O Lord,
  ⁹ All the nations that you have made will come and worship before you and
  glorify your name;
  ¹⁰ You are great and do wondrous things;
  You alone are God.
¹¹ O LORD,
  Teach me your ways that I may walk in your truth;
  Unite my heart to fear your name.
¹² O Lord my God,
  I will praise you with all my heart; and
  I will glorify your name forevermore;
    ¹³ For great is your lovingkindness toward me,
    For you have delivered my soul from the depths of Sheol.

---

a Literally, "abounding in."

[14] O God,

> Arrogant men have risen against me, and
> A band of violent men have sought my life;
> And they have not set you before them.

[15] But you, O Lord, are a God *who is*

> Merciful,
> Gracious,
> Slow to anger, and
> Abounding in lovingkindness and truth.

[16] Turn to me;

Have mercy on me;

Give your strength to your servant,

Save the son of your maidservant;

[17] Show me a sign of your favor;

> That those who hate me will see it and be ashamed;
> > Because you, LORD, have helped me and comforted me.

Psalm 87
Celebrating Zion

A psalm. A song of the sons of Korah.

[1] His foundation, *Jerusalem*, is on the holy mountain.

[2] The LORD loves the gates of Zion[a] more than all the *other* cities[b] in Jacob.

[3] O city of God, what glorious things are said about you.   Selah

[4] For instance,[c]

> "*The people of* Rahab and Babylon are among those who know of me."
> *The people of* Philistia, Tyre and *even* Cush, *say* "This one was born there."

[5] Regarding Zion it will be said,

> "This one and that one were born there," and
> "The Most High himself will establish her."

[6] The LORD *himself* records in the register of peoples, "This man was born in Jerusalem."[d]   Selah

[7] Singers and the dancers *will declare:* "All my fountains[e] of joy are in you."

---

a   "Gates of Zion": a metaphor for Jerusalem.
b   Literally, "dwellings."
c   Literally, "I mention."
d   Literally, "there."
e   Or "my springs"; a metaphor for the source of life. Israel is a semi-arid region.

Psalm 88
Cry of the Distressed

A psalm and song of the sons of Korah.
To the music director: to the tune of "The Suffering of Affliction."
A maskil of[a] Heman the Ezrahite.

¹ O Lord, God of my salvation,
  I have cried day and night before you.
² Let my prayer come before you;
  Incline your ear to my cry.
³ For:

> My soul is full of troubles;
> My life draws near to the grave;[b]
>   ⁴ I am counted with those who go down into the pit;
>   I have become a person who has no strength;
>   ⁵ I am forsaken
>   Like the dead,
>   Like those lying in the grave
>   Whom you remember no more,
>   Who are cut off from your *caring* hand.

⁶ You have laid me in the lowest pit, in darkness, in the depths;
⁷ Your wrath lies heavily upon me;
  You have overwhelmed me with all your waves;   Selah
⁸ You have removed my friends, made me repulsive to them;
  I am shut in and cannot escape;
⁹ My eyes grow dim because of my affliction.

O Lord,
  I have called upon you daily;
  I have stretched out my hands to you.
    ¹⁰ Will you show wonders to the dead?
    Will the dead arise and praise you?   Selah
      ¹¹ Will your lovingkindness be declared in the grave?
      Will your faithfulness *be declared* in *the place of* destruction?
        ¹² Will your wonders *be known* in the dark?
        Will your righteousness be known in the land of forgetfulness?
¹³ O Lord,
  I am crying out to you *now*,
  And my prayer will come before you in the morning *too*.

¹⁴ O Lord,
  Why do you reject me?
  Why do you hide your face from me?

---

a   Or "for."
b   Literally, "to Sheol."

¹⁵ I have been afflicted and close to death since my youth;
I am perplexed while I suffer your terrors;
¹⁶ Your wrath sweeps over me;
Your terrors destroy me, ¹⁷ daily surround me like water, completely engulf me;
¹⁸ You have removed my lover and my friends from me;
Darkness is my acquaintance.

Psalm 89
Singing Praise When in Turmoil

Maskil of Ethan the Ezrahite.

¹ I will sing of the lovingkindness of the LORD forever;
I will make known your faithfulness to all generations with my mouth;
² I will declare,
"*Your* lovingkindness stands forever;
Your faithfulness is established in the heavens."

You said,
³ "I have made a covenant with my chosen one;
I have sworn to my servant David:
⁴ 'I will establish your descendants forever,
And build up your throne through all generations.'"   Selah

⁵ O LORD,
The heavens praise your wonder and faithfulness in the assembly of the holy ones, for
⁶ Who in the skies can be compared to the LORD?
Who among the heavenly beings is like the LORD God,
⁷ A God greatly feared in the council of the holy *beings*,
Held in awe by all who are around him?
⁸ O LORD God of hosts,
Who is strong like you?
O LORD,
Your faithfulness surrounds you;
⁹ You rule the raging of the sea—when its waves rise, you still them;
¹⁰ You crushed Rahab like she was a corpse;ᵃ and
You scattered your enemies with your mighty arm.

¹¹ The heavens are yours;
The earth also is yours;
The world and all that is in it—you created it *all*.
¹² The north and the south—you created them;
Mt. Tabor and Mt. Hermon praise your name.

---

a   Literally, "like one slain."

¹³ You have a mighty arm;
Your *left* hand is strong and your right hand is lifted high.
¹⁴ Righteousness and justice are the foundation of your throne;
Lovingkindness and truth go before you.

¹⁵ Blessed are the people who
Know the joyful sound;^{*a*}
Walk, O Lord, in the light of your presence;
¹⁶ Rejoice in your name all day long; and
Exalt in your righteousness.
¹⁷ You are their glory and their strength, and
And by your favor our strength is increased.^{*b*}
(¹⁸ Indeed, the Lord is our defense, and The Holy One of Israel is our king.)

¹⁹ Once you spoke in vision to your godly people and said,
"I have given help to one who is mighty;
I have exalted a young man from among the people;
²⁰ I have found David, my servant, and anointed him with my holy oil.
²¹ He will be established by my hand; and also,
My arm will strengthen him.
²² The enemy will not exact *tribute* from him;
Nor will the son of wickedness overwhelm him.
²³ I will crush his foes before his face
And strike down those who hate him.
²⁴ My faithfulness and my lovingkindness will be with him, and
Through my name his strength^{*c*} will be exalted;
²⁵ I will set his hand over the sea, his right hand over the rivers.
²⁶ He will cry to me, 'You are my Father, my God, the rock of my salvation.'
²⁷ I will make him my firstborn, highest of the kings of the earth.
²⁸ I will maintain my lovingkindness for him forever;
My covenant with him will stand firm;
²⁹ I will establish his family line forever;
And his throne as the days of heaven.
³⁰ If his children
Forsake my law,
Do not walk in my judgments,
³¹ Break my statutes, and
Do not keep my commandments;
³² Then I will punish their transgression with the rod, their iniquity with flogging.
³³ Nevertheless, I will not
Take my lovingkindness from them,
Deal falsely, but be faithful,^{*d*}

---

a Hebrew: "teruah," which is the sounding of the ram's horn at festival times.
b Literally, "our horn is lifted."
c Literally, "horn."
d Literally, "deal falsely with my faithfulness."

³⁴ Break my covenant, or
    Alter what went out of my lips.
³⁵ Once *for all time* I swore an oath by my holiness—and I will not lie to
    David—that
    ³⁶ His descendants will continue forever, and
        His throne will be as the sun before me—³⁷ established forever like
        the moon *is established as* a faithful witness *to the sun's presence* in the
        sky."   Selah

³⁸ But you, *God*, have:
    Cast *him* off and rejected *him*;
    Been enraged with your anointed;
    ³⁹ Renounced your covenant with your servant;
    Profaned his crown *by casting* it to the ground;
⁴⁰ Broken down all his walls;
    Brought his strongholds to ruin;
    (⁴¹ All who pass by plunder him. He is the scorn of his neighbors.)
⁴² Strengthened the right hand of his adversaries;
    (All his enemies rejoice!)
⁴³ Turned aside the edge of his sword;
    (He cannot stand in battle!)
⁴⁴ Put an end to his glory;
    Cast his throne down to the ground;
⁴⁵ Shortened the days of his youth;*ᵃ* and
    Covered him with shame.   Selah

⁴⁶ How long, O LORD?
    Will you hide yourself from us forever?
    Will your wrath burn like fire?
⁴⁷ Remember how short our life is.
    Why have you created the children of man in vain?
    ⁴⁸ What man can live and never see death?
    Who can deliver his soul from the power of Sheol?   Selah
⁴⁹ Lord, where is your former lovingkindness that in your faithfulness you swore to
    David?
⁵⁰ Take note, Lord,
    How your servant is mocked;
    How I bear in my heart the insults of all the *heathen* nations;
    ⁵¹ With which your enemies have mocked us, O LORD;
    With which they have mocked the footsteps of your anointed *king*.

Closing Doxology

⁵² Blessed be the LORD forever.
    Amen, and amen.

---

a   A metaphor for aging prematurely.

Psalm 90
Establish Us, Though We Are Little

A prayer of Moses, the man of God.

¹ Lord, you have been our dwelling place
　　Throughout all generations,
　　² Before the mountains were brought forth,
　　Before you formed the earth and the world,
　　From everlasting to everlasting.
You are God.
　　³ You turn man back into dust,
　　　Saying, "Return *to dust*, you children of men."
　　⁴ For a thousand years in your sight are
　　　Like yesterday when it has passed,
　　　Like a watch in the night.
　　⁵ You sweep *man* away like a flood.
　　　They are *as fleeting* as a dream;
　　　They are *as temporary as* grass that springs up in the morning.
　　　　⁶ In the morning it springs up and flourishes;
　　　　In the evening it lies down and withers.
　　　⁷ We are consumed by your anger, and
　　　We are troubled by your wrath.
　　⁸ You have set our iniquities before you;
　　Our secrets are *exposed* in the light of your presence.
　　⁹ All our days pass away under your wrath.
　　We finish our years with a groan.
　　　¹⁰ The days of our life are seventy years;
　　　Or perhaps they may be eighty years due to *one's* strength;
　　　But they are *all only* ^a pride, labor and sorrow.
　　They soon pass, and we fly away.
¹¹ Who can comprehend
　　The power of your anger,
　　Your fearsomeness,
　　Your fury?
¹² So teach us to number our days, that we may get a heart of wisdom.

¹³ O LORD,
　　Come back; how long *will it be?*
　　Have pity on your servants.
　　¹⁴ Satisfy us in the morning with your lovingkindness,
　　　That we may rejoice and be glad all of our days;

---

a　Or "their span is only." The Hebrew is not clear.

¹⁵ Make us glad

> For as many days as you have afflicted us,
> For as many years as we have seen evil.

¹⁶ Show your work to your servants;
Show your majesty to our children.

¹⁷ Let the favor of the LORD our God be upon us;
Make firm the work of our hands;
Yes, establish the work of our hands.

Psalm 91
Abiding in the Shadow of the Almighty

¹ He who dwells in the shelter of the Most High will abide *a* in the shadow of the Almighty.

² I will say to the LORD,
> "My refuge and my fortress;
> My God in whom I trust."

³ For

> He will deliver you from the trapper's snare and the deadly pestilence;
> ⁴ He will cover you with his feathers,
>> And under his wings you will find refuge;
> His faithfulness will be your shield and protection. *b*

⁵ You will not be afraid
> Of the terror by night;
> Of the arrow that flies by day;
> ⁶ Of the pestilence that stalks in the darkness; or
> Of the destruction that ravages at midday.
>> ⁷ A thousand may fall at your side and ten thousand at your right hand,
>> but harm *c* will not come near you.

⁸ You will look with your eyes and see the reward of the wicked,
> ⁹ Because you have made the LORD Most High your place of protection,
> your shelter.

¹⁰ No evil will come upon you;
No plague will come upon your dwelling;
> ¹¹ For he will give his angels charge over you
>> To guard in all your ways,
>>> ¹² To hold you up with their hands so you will not strike your foot against
>>> a stone.

¹³ You will tread upon lions and cobras;
You will trample the young lion and the serpent under your feet.

---

a   Or "will rest."
b   Or "and buckler." "Buckler": a small shield strapped over the arm.
c   Literally, "it."

The Lord says:

¹⁴ "I will deliver him because he loves me;ᵃ
I will protectᵇ him because he knows my name.
¹⁵ He will call upon me,
And I will:

Answer him,
Be with him in trouble,
Deliver him,
Honor him,
¹⁶ Satisfy him with long life, and
Show him my salvation."

Psalm 92
A Sabbath Song

A psalm. A song for the Sabbath day.

¹ It is good
To give thanks to the LORD;
To sing praises to your name, O Most High;
² To proclaim
Your lovingkindness in the morning and
Your faithfulness at night
³ Upon a ten-stringed harp,
To the melody of the harp and lyre.
⁴ For you, LORD, have made me glad through your work.
I will sing joyfully of the works of your hands.

⁵ O LORD,
How great are your works.
How profoundᶜ are your thoughts.
⁶ A senseless man cannot know;
A stupid man does not understand this:
⁷ Though the wicked spring up like grass and
Though all who do iniquity flourish;
They will be destroyed ultimately.ᵈ
⁸ You, O LORD, are on highᵉ forever.
⁹ For, lo, your enemies, O LORD;
For, lo, your enemies will perish.
All the workers of iniquity will be scattered.

---

a   Or "holds fast to me."
b   Literally, "set."
c   Literally, "very deep."
d   Literally, "be destroyed forever."
e   Or "exalted."

^{10} You have built up my strength^a like that of a wild ox;
You have anointed me with fresh oil;^{b}
^{11} My eyes look *triumphantly* at my foes;
And my ears hear the *cries of* my enemies who rise up against me.

^{12} The righteous will flourish like the palm tree;
They will grow like the cedars of Lebanon;
^{13} Those who are planted in the house of the LORD will flourish in the courts of our
God.
^{14} They will bear fruit in old age, *still* green and full *of sap.*
^{15} They will declare,
"The LORD is upright,
He is my rock, and
There is no unrighteousness in him."

Psalm 93
The Lord Reigns

^{1} The LORD reigns.
He is robed with majesty;
Indeed, the LORD is robed in majesty and armed^c with strength.
His world is established and cannot be shaken.^{d}

^{2} LORD,
Your throne was established long ago;
You are from eternity.
^{3} The oceans have risen up, O LORD;
The oceans have lifted up their voice;
The oceans lift up their pounding *waves.*
^{4} But the LORD on high is mightier than the noise of many waters;
Yes, than the mighty waves of the sea.

^{5} Your law stands firm.
Holiness suits your house, O LORD, forever.

Psalm 94
A Call for God's Vengeance

^{1} O LORD God of vengeance;
God of vengeance:
Shine;

---

a Literally, "horn"
b Or "you have poured fresh oil on me."
c Literally, "and belted."
d Or "be moved."

² Rise up, O judge of the earth;
Pay back the proud what they deserve.
³ O Lᴏʀᴅ, how long will the wicked ...
How long will the wicked gloat?
⁴ How long will they pour out arrogant words?
How long will all those who do iniquity boast?
⁵ O Lᴏʀᴅ, they
Crush your people,
Afflict your heritage,
⁶ Kill widows and foreigners, and
Murder the fatherless.
⁷ They say,,
"The Lᴏʀᴅ will not see,
Nor will the God of Jacob pay attention to it."

But I say,
⁸ Pay attention, you senseless people, you fools.
When will you understand?
⁹ He who implanted the ear, doesn't he hear?
He who formed the eye, doesn't he see?
¹⁰ He who disciplines the *heathen* nations, won't he correct *you?*
He who teaches man knowledge, *doesn't he know?*
¹¹ The Lᴏʀᴅ knows the thoughts of man, that they are *only* breath.

¹² Lᴏʀᴅ,
Blessed is the man whom you discipline, whom you teach out of your law;
¹³ That you grant him rest*ᵃ* in the days of adversity until a pit is dug for the wicked.

¹⁴ The Lᴏʀᴅ will not forsake his people;
He will not forsake his inheritance.
¹⁵ Judgment will become righteous again,
And all the upright of heart will follow it.

¹⁶ Who will rise up with me against the wicked?
Who will stand up with me against wickedness?
¹⁷ If the Lᴏʀᴅ hadn't been my help,
Soon my soul would have dwelt in silence;
¹⁸ When I cried, "My foot is slipping!"
Your lovingkindness, O Lᴏʀᴅ, held me up.
¹⁹ Though a multitude of anxious thoughts are within me,
Your consoling *words* delight my soul.

²⁰ Can wicked rulers,*ᵇ* those who devise and decree mischief, be allied with God?

---

a   Or "grant him relief."
b   Literally, "the throne of destruction."

21 *No*, they are united against the life of the righteous and condemn the innocent to death.

22 The LORD is my fortress;
God is the rock of my refuge.
23 He will bring their wickedness upon them;
He will destroy them for their evil *deeds*;
The LORD our God will destroy them.

Psalm 95
Come, Let Us Sing to the Lord

1 Come,
Let us sing to the LORD;
Let us shout to the rock of our salvation;
2 Let us come before his presence with thanksgiving;
Let us shout to him with psalms;
3 For the LORD is
A great God, and
A great King above all gods.
4 The depths of the earth are in his hands;
The peaks of the mountains *too*;
5 The sea is his, for he made it; and
His hands formed the dry land.
6 Come,
Let us worship and bow down;
Let us kneel before the LORD, our maker;
7 For he is our God; and
We are the people of his pasture, sheep under his *caring* hand.

If only you would hear his voice today, *saying*:
8 "Do not harden your heart
As at Meribah[a] and
As in the day of Massah[b] in the wilderness
9 When your fathers tempted me and tried me even though they had seen my works.
10 For forty years I was grieved by that generation, and thought,
'This is a people who err[c] in their heart.
They have not known my ways.'
11 Therefore I swore in my wrath: 'They shall not enter into my rest.'"

---

a "Meribah" means provocation. A reference to Ex. 17:7
b "Massah" means temptation. A reference to Ex. 17:7.
c Or "go astray."

Psalm 96
Sing and Worship the Lord

¹ Sing a new song to the LORD;
Sing to the LORD, all the earth;
² Sing to the LORD;
Bless his name;
Proclaim his salvation day after day;
³ Declare his glory among the *heathen* nations;
Declare his wonders among all people *like this:*
  ⁴ "The LORD is great, and greatly to be praised;
    He is to be feared above all gods,
      ⁵ For all the gods of *other* people are *only* idols.
    The LORD made the heavens.
  ⁶ Splendor and majesty are before him;
    Strength and beauty *fill*^a his sanctuary."

⁷ Give credit to the LORD, you families of his people;
    Recognize the Lord's glory and strength;
  ⁸ Give to the Lord the glory due his name.
Bring an offering and come into his courts;
⁹ Worship the LORD in the splendor of his holiness;
Tremble before him, all the earth;
¹⁰ Tell^b the *heathen* nations,
    "The LORD reigns.
    Indeed, the world stands firm *by him;* it will not be moved.
    He will judge all people fairly."

¹¹ Let the heavens be glad;
Let the earth rejoice;
Let the sea and everything in it roar *with joy;*
¹² Let the field and everything in it sing with joy.
Then all the trees of the forest will rejoice ¹³ before the LORD, for
  ¹³ He is coming, coming to judge the earth.
  He will judge the world with righteousness, the people by his truth.^c

Psalm 97
Rejoice and Be Glad God Reigns

¹ The LORD reigns.
Let the earth rejoice;
Let many coastlands rejoice.

---

a Or "are in."
b Literally, "say among."
c Or "in his faithfulness."

² Clouds and darkness surround him;
Righteousness and justice are the foundation of his throne;
³ A fire goes before him and burns up his enemies on every side;
⁴ His lightning lights up the world.

The earth sees and trembles;
⁵ The hills melt like wax before the LORD, before the Lord of the whole earth;
⁶ The heavens proclaim his righteousness;
All people see his glory.

⁷ Shame on all who worship carved *images* and boast about idols.
Worship him, all you gods!

⁸ O LORD,

Zion hears and is glad;
The daughters*ᵃ* of Judah rejoice because of your judgments.
⁹ For you, LORD, are the Most High above all the earth;
You are exalted far above all gods.

¹⁰ You who love the LORD, hate evil.
For

He preserves the lives of his godly ones;
He delivers them from the hand of the wicked; and
¹¹ He sheds light upon the righteous, joy upon the upright in heart.
¹² You who are righteous,
Rejoice in the LORD;
Praise his holy name.

Psalm 98
Sing and Make a Joyful Noise

A psalm.

¹ Sing a new song to the Lord,
For he has done marvelous things.
His right hand and his holy arm have won the victory;
² The LORD has made his salvation known;
He has revealed his righteousness in the sight of the nations;
³ He has remembered his lovingkindness and his faithfulness toward the house of Israel;
All the ends of the earth have seen the salvation of our God.

⁴ All the earth:
Shout joyfully to the Lord;
Burst forth, sing for joy, sing praises;
⁵ Sing to the LORD with the harp, the lyre, melodious sounds ⁶and trumpets;

---

a   Or "villages."

Sound the ram's horn;
Shout joyfully before the LORD, the King.
⁷ Let the sea and everything in it roar *his praise;*
The world *too,* and all who live in it;
⁸ Let the rivers clap their hands;
Let the hills sing together for joy ⁹ before the LORD,
For he is coming to judge the earth.
He will judge the world righteously, the people fairly.

Psalm 99
Exalt the Lord, For He Is Holy

¹ The LORD reigns;
Let the people tremble.
He sits enthroned between the cherubims;
Let the earth quake.
² The LORD is great in Zion, exalted above all the people;
³ Let them praise his*ᵃ* great and awesome name.
He is holy.
⁴ The king is mighty;
He loves justice.
Lord, you establish fairness, carry out justice and righteousness in Jacob.
⁵ Exalt the LORD our God;
Worship at his footstool.
He is holy.

Historical Note

⁶ Moses and Aaron were among his priests, and
Samuel was among those who called upon his name.
They called upon the LORD, and he answered them.
⁷ He spoke to them from the pillar of cloud.
They obeyed his statutes, the decrees that he gave them.
⁸ O LORD our God,
You answered them;
You were a God who forgave;
Yet you did avenge their sinful deeds.

---

⁹ Exalt the LORD our God;
Worship at his holy mountain.
The LORD our God is holy.

---

a Literally, "your."

Psalm 100
A Psalm of Thanksgiving

A psalm of Thanksgiving

1 Shout joyfully to the Lord, all *people of* the earth;
2 Worship*ᵃ* the Lᴏʀᴅ with gladness;
  Come into his presence with singing;
3 Know that the Lᴏʀᴅ himself is God;
      He made us—we're his,*ᵇ* his people, the sheep of his pasture.
4 Enter into his gates with thanksgiving, into his courts with praise;
  Give thanks to him and
  Bless his name.

5 The Lᴏʀᴅ is good;
  His mercy endures forever; and
  His faithfulness continues through all generations.

Psalm 101
Pledge of the Faithful

A psalm of David

1 I will sing of lovingkindness and justice;
      To you, O Lᴏʀᴅ, I will sing.
2 I will ponder the blameless way—when will you come to me?
  I will walk in my house with integrity in my heart;
3 I will set no wicked*ᶜ* thing before my eyes,
      For I hate deeds outside *of your law.*
          They will not cling to me, and
              4 The perverse*ᵈ* heart will depart from me.
  I will not know evil;
5 I will destroy whoever secretly slanders his neighbor; and
  I will not tolerate anyone who has a haughty look and a proud heart.

6 My eyes will look with favor*ᵉ* on the faithful of the land,
      That they may dwell with me.
  Those who walk in a blameless way will minister to me;
7 Those who practice deceit will not dwell within my house;
  Whoever tells lies will not stay in my sight;
8 Every morning I will
      Destroy all the wicked of the land and
      Cut off all evildoers from the city of the Lᴏʀᴅ.

---

a   Literally, "serve."
b   Or "and not we ourselves."
c   Literally, "worthless."
d   "Perverse": persisting in error, turned from right and good.
e   Or "eyes will be on."

Psalm 102
Prayer of the Overwhelmed

A prayer of the afflicted. For *when a person is* overwhelmed and pours out his complaint before the Lord.

¹ O Lord,
    Hear my prayer;
    Let my cry come to you;
    ² Don't hide your face from me in the day of my distress;
    Incline your ear to me;
    Answer me quickly on this day I am calling.
³ For:
    My days end up as smoke;
    My bones burn, are charred like charcoal;[a]
    ⁴ My heart is crushed, withered like grass—such that I forget to eat my food!
    ⁵ My bones cleave to my skin because of my loud groaning;
    ⁶ I am like a pelican in the desert;
    I am like an owl in the wastelands;
    ⁷ I lie awake, like a bird alone on a housetop;
    ⁸ My enemies taunt me, celebrate *my misery* and curse me all day long;
    ⁹ I eat ashes for food and mix my drink with *tears from* crying
      ¹⁰ Because of your indignation and your anger;
      For you had lifted me up, and *now* you have cast me down.
    ¹¹ My days are like an evening shadow;
    I am withering away like grass.

¹² O LORD,
    You are enthroned forever;
    You are remembered throughout all generations;
    ¹³ You will rise up and have mercy on Zion.
      The time to favor her, the appointed time, has come;
      ¹⁴ For *now* your servants
        Hold dear the stones *from her destroyed walls and*
        Are moved to pity by the dust *of her streets.*
    ¹⁵ Let the *heathen* nations fear the name of the LORD;
    Let all the kings of the earth *fear* your glory.

¹⁶ When the LORD rebuilds Zion,
    He will appear in his glory;
    ¹⁷ He will regard the prayer of the destitute;
    He will not despise their prayers.
¹⁸ Let this be written for the generation to come,
    So the people yet to be born will praise the LORD.

---

a   Literally, "a burning burning [sic] mass"

¹⁹ *Write,*

"He has looked down from the height of his sanctuary;
The LORD in heaven has looked upon the earth
  ²⁰ To hear the groaning of the prisoner,
    To set free those who are condemned to death;
      ²¹ That the name of the LORD will be proclaimed[a] in Zion, his praise
        proclaimed in Jerusalem;
          ²² When the people and the kingdoms are gathered together to serve
            the LORD."

²³ He broke my strength in the midcourse *of my life;*
He shortened my days.
²⁴ So I said:

"O my God, don't take me away in the midst of my days.
Your years *are throughout* all generations.
  ²⁵ Long ago you laid the foundation of the earth;
  The heavens are the work of your hands.
    ²⁶ They will perish, but you will continue;
    All of these things will wear out like a garment;
    You will change them like clothing; and
    They will pass away.
    ²⁷ But you are *always* the same,
    And your years will have no end."

²⁸ The children of your servants will dwell securely,
And their descendants will be established in your presence.

Psalm 103
Bless the Lord

A psalm of David

¹ Bless the LORD, O my soul, and all that is within me, bless his holy name.
² Bless the LORD, O my soul, and do not forget all his benefits:
  ³ Who forgives all your sins;
  Who heals all your diseases;
  ⁴ Who redeems your life from the pit;
  Who crowns you with lovingkindness and compassion;
  ⁵ Who satisfies your years with good things,
    So that your youth is renewed like a *soaring* eagle.
⁶ The LORD carries out righteousness and justice for all who are oppressed.
⁷ He made his ways known to Moses;
He *made* his acts *known* to the children of Israel.

---

a Literally, "told."

[8] The LORD is
> Compassionate and gracious,
> Slow to anger, and
> Abounding in lovingkindness.

[9] He will not always chide,[a]
Nor will he hold on to his anger forever.

[10] He has not dealt with us as our sins deserve,[b]
Nor has he repaid us in proportion to[c] our iniquities.
> [11] For as high as the heavens are above the earth,
>> That's how great his lovingkindness is toward those who fear him.
> [12] As far as the east is from the west,
>> That's how far he has removed our transgressions from us.
> [13] Like a father has compassion on his children,
>> That's how the LORD has compassion on those who fear him.

[14] For he knows what we are made of,[d] remembers that we are dust.

[15] As for man,
> His days are like grass;
> He flourishes like a flower in a field:
>> [16] When the wind passes over it, it is no more;
>> And the place *where it was* no longer knows *that it ever was.*

[17] But the lovingkindness of the LORD is over those who fear him from everlasting to everlasting,
And his righteousness is with their children's children;
> [18] To those who keep his covenant, who remember his commandments[e] and keep them.[f]

[19] The LORD has established his throne in the heavens,
And his sovereignty rules over everything.

[20] Bless the LORD, you his angels
> Who are mighty in strength;
> Who do his bidding,[g] and
> Who obey the voice of his word.

[21] Bless the LORD, all you his hosts,
> You his servants who do his will.

[22] Bless the LORD, all his works in all places of his dominion;
Bless the LORD, O my soul.

---

a   "Chide":to voice disapproval, speak out angrily.
b   Literally, "with us according to our sins."
c   Literally, "rewarded us according to."
d   Literally, "knows our form."
e   Or "live by his precepts."
f   Literally, "to do them."
g   Literally, "his word."

Psalm 104
Blessing God and Praising His Works

[1] Bless the LORD, O my soul.
O LORD my God,
>You are very great;
>You
>>Are clothed with splendor and majesty,
>>>[2] Covering yourself with a garment of light;
>>Stretch out the heavens like a tent *over us;*
>>[3] Lay the rafters of your chambers in the rain clouds;[a]
>>Make the clouds your chariot and ride upon the wings of the wind;
>>[4] Make the winds your messengers, flaming fire your servants.

[5] You set the earth on its foundation so it will never totter, and
[6] You covered it with deep *waters* as with a garment.
>(The waters
>>Stood above the mountains;
>>>[7] Fled at your rebuke;
>>Hurried away at your thunder;
>>>[8] Rose over the mountains; and then they
>>Sank into the valleys and the places you made for them.
>>[9] You set a boundary they cannot cross;
>>They will never again cover the earth.)
[10] You send the springs flowing between the hills into the valleys.
>[11] They give *water* to every beast of the field.
>*Even* wild donkeys quench their thirst.
>[12] The birds of the air[b] dwell above them, singing among the branches.
[13] You water the hills from your upper chambers *such that* the earth is satisfied
by the fruit of your work.
[14] You make
>Grass grow for the cattle;
>Plants *grow* to be cultivated by man to produce food from the earth;
>>[15] Wine to make the heart of man glad;
>>Oil to make his face shine; and
>>Food to strengthen[c] man's heart.
[16] The trees of the LORD are watered well,
>*Like* the cedars of Lebanon that he planted [17]in which birds make nests.
>*Like* the cypress trees in which storks *make* their homes.
[18] The high mountains are for wild goats, and
The rocks are a refuge for hyraxes.[d]

---

a   Literally, "in the waters."
b   Or "of the heavens."
c   Or "to sustain."
d   "Hyrax": an animal resembling a woodchuck.

¹⁹ You make the moon *mark* time;
The sun—you appoint its time to set.ᵃ
²⁰ You appoint *the time for* darkness.
When it becomes night, all the beasts of the forest creep about. ²¹ The young lions roar for their prey and seek their food from God. ²² When the sun rises, they withdraw and lie down in their dens. ²³ Then man goes out to his work and labors until evening.

²⁴ O LORD, how many are your works.
In wisdom you have made them all;
The earth is full of your creations:ᵇ
²⁵ The great and wide sea with numberless swarms of big and small creatures;
²⁶ The ships *on it;* and
The monstrous sea creaturesᶜ you created to play in it.

²⁷ They all wait upon you to give them their food in due season;
²⁸ When you give it to them, they gather it up;
When you open your hand, they are filled with good things;
²⁹ When you hide your face, they are dismayed;
When you take away their breath, they die and return to dust;
³⁰ When you send out your spirit,ᵈ they are created.
You renew the face of the earth.

³¹ The glory of the LORD will continue forever;
The LORD will rejoice in his works.
³² He looks on the earth, and it trembles;
He touches the hills, and they smoke.

³³ I will sing to the Lord as long as I live;
I will sing praises to my God as long asᵉ I have life.
³⁴ My meditation of him will be sweet;
For I rejoice in the LORD.

³⁵ But may sinners vanishᶠ from the earth;
Let the wicked be no more.
Bless the LORD, O my soul;
Hallelujah!

---

a   Literally, "the sun knows its setting."
b   Literally, "your possessions."
c   Hebrew: "Leviathan." A reference to large sea creatures.
d   Or "your breath."
e   Literally, "praise to God while I have life."
f   Literally, "be consumed."

Psalm 105
Making Known the Deeds of the Lord

¹ O give thanks to the Lord;
Call upon his name;
Make his deeds known among the people;
² Sing to him; sing praises to him;
Tell of all his wondrous works;
³ Glory in his holy name;
Let the hearts of those who seek the LORD rejoice.

⁴ Seek the LORD;
Seek his strength;
Seek his face continually.
⁵ Remember the marvelous works he has done,
His wonders and the judgments *spoken* by his mouth.

Consider How God Remembers His Covenant

⁶ O you descendants of his servant Abraham,
O you children of Jacob, his chosen *ones*:
⁷ He is the LORD our God;
His judgments are throughout the earth;
⁸ He forever remembers his covenant
(*i.e.,* The words he commanded to a thousand generations:
⁹ The *covenant* he made with Abraham;
His oath to Isaac;
¹⁰ Which he confirmed as a decree to Jacob;
And confirmed as an everlasting covenant to Israel
¹¹ When he said, "I will give you the land of Canaan as your portion for an inheritance";
¹² When they were few in number, few and strangers *in the land;*
¹³ When they wandered from nation to nation, from *one* kingdom to another.*ᵃ*)
¹⁴ He allowed no man to oppress them.
He *even* rebuked kings for their sakes,
¹⁵ Saying, "Do not touch my anointed ones or harm my prophets."
¹⁶ He called for a famine upon the land *of Canaan* and destroyed*ᵇ* the whole supply of food.
¹⁷ He sent a man before them, Joseph.
He was sold for a slave;
¹⁸ His feet were hurt*ᶜ* by shackles;

---

a Literally, "to another people."
b Literally, "he broke."
c Literally, "afflicted."

His *neck* was put in an iron *collar*
   ¹⁹ Until the time that his prophecy was fulfilled*ᵃ*
      (*i.e.,* the word of the Lord that tested his character*ᵇ*).
   ²⁰ The king sent for and released him;
   The ruler of the *Egyptian* people let him go free;
   ²¹ The king made him lord of his house and ruler of all his possessions,
      ²² *Even* to imprison*ᶜ* his princes as he wished, and
      To teach his advisors*ᵈ* wisdom.

²³ Then Israel came into Egypt,
   And Jacob lived temporarily in the land of Ham.
²⁴ *The Lord* made his people bear many children,*ᵉ* made them stronger than
   their enemies;
²⁵ Then he turned their *enemies'* hearts to hate his people,
   And they dealt deceitfully with his servants.
²⁶ Then he sent his servant Moses, and Aaron whom he had chosen; and
²⁷ They performed his signs among *the Egyptians*—miracles in the land of Ham.
   ²⁸ He sent darkness and made it dark, for they had rebelled*ᶠ* against his
      words.
   ²⁹ He turned their waters into blood, *causing* their fish to die.
   ³⁰ Then frogs swarmed their land, even into the chambers of their rulers.
   ³¹ He spoke, and swarms *of flies* came; and gnats *filled* all their country.
   ³² He gave them hail instead of rain, and lightning fired*ᵍ* over their land.
   ³³ He struck down their vines and fig trees, and shattered the trees of their
      country.
   ³⁴ He spoke, and innumerable young locusts came ³⁵ and ate up all the
      plants in their land—devouring the fruit of their land.
   ³⁶ He struck down all the firstborn *sons* in their land, the first fruits of all
      their manhood.*ʰ*
   ³⁷ He brought out Israel with silver and gold, and no one among their tribes
      stumbled.
   ³⁸ Egypt was glad when they departed, because dread of Israel had fallen
      upon them.

³⁹ He spread out a cloud for a covering, and fire to light the night.
⁴⁰ They asked *for meat,*
   And he brought quails;
   And satisfied them with *manna,* the bread of heaven.

---

a   Literally, "time that his word came to pass."
b   Literally, "tested him."
c   Literally, "to bind."
d   Literally, "elders," or "princes."
e   Literally, "his people be fruitful."
f   Literally, "for hadn't they rebelled."
g   Literally, "flaming fire."
h   Literally, "all their vigor."

⁴¹ He opened the rock, and the water gushed out and flowed in the desert like a river.

⁴² Because he remembered his holy promise and his servant Abraham,*ᵃ*

⁴³ He brought out his people with joy, his chosen with joyful *singing*;

⁴⁴ He gave them the lands of the *heathen* peoples;

And they took the *fruit of the* labor of those people

⁴⁵ That they might observe his statutes and keep his laws.

Hallelujah!

Psalm 106
Israel's Unfaithfulness, God's Faithfulness

¹ Hallelujah!
Give thanks to the Lord;
For he is good;
For his lovingkindness is everlasting.

² Who can *adequately* proclaim the mighty acts of the LORD?
Who can proclaim all his praises?
³ Blessed are those who practice justice,
And those who do what is right all the time.

⁴ O LORD,
Remember me, with the favor *you show* to your people;
Visit me with your salvation ⁵ that I may
See the prosperity of your chosen *people*;
Rejoice in the gladness of your nation; and
Glory in your inheritance;
⁶ *Though* we have
Sinned like our ancestors,
Committed iniquity, and
Behaved wickedly.

⁷ Our fathers did not understand *the reason for* his miracles in Egypt;*ᵇ*
They did not remember the abundance of his lovingkindness;
But rebelled by the sea, the Red Sea.
⁸ *Nevertheless*, he
Saved them for his name's sake,
That he might make his mighty power to be known;
⁹ Rebuked the Red Sea and dried it up;
Led them through its depths as through a desert;

---

a Or "holy promise to his servant Abraham."
b See Psalm 105:45.

¹⁰ Saved them from the hand of those who hated them; and
Redeemed them from the hand of the enemy.
(¹¹ The waters covered their enemies. Not one was left.)
¹² Then they believed his words;
Then they sang his praise.

¹³ But they soon forgot his works;
They did not wait for his counsel;
¹⁴ But *craved* pleasure exceedingly in the wilderness;
And put God to the test^a in the desert.
¹⁵ So he gave them what they asked for by sending a wasting *disease* upon them.^b
¹⁶ In the camp they envied Moses and Aaron, the holy one of the LORD,
¹⁷ So the earth opened and swallowed up Dathan and buried the companions of Abiram;
¹⁸ And fire broke out among their followers, and flames burned up the wicked.
¹⁹ They made a calf in Horeb^c and worshipped the molten metal *image*.
²⁰ Thus they exchanged their glory (*i.e., the Lord*) for an image of an ox that eats grass!
²¹ They forgot God, their savior, who had done
Great things in Egypt;
²² Wondrous works in the land of Ham; and
Awesome deeds at the Red Sea.
²³ Therefore, he said that he would destroy them;
Except that Moses, his chosen, stood before him in the breach
To turn away his wrath from destroying them.
²⁴ Then they despised the pleasant land;
They did not believe his promise^d *to care for them*;
²⁵ They grumbled in their tents and did not listen to the voice of the LORD.
²⁶ Therefore he lifted up his hand against them;
Made them fall^e in the wilderness,
²⁷ Cast their descendants among the *heathen* nations, and
Scattered them throughout their lands.

²⁸ Then they yoked themselves to Baal of Peor^f—ate sacrifices offered to a lifeless *image*!
²⁹ They provoked him to anger with their deeds,
And the plague broke out upon them.
³⁰ Then Phinehas stood up and intervened,

---

a Literally, "tempted God."
b Literally, "upon their soul."
c Aka, Mt. Sinai..
d Literally, "word."
e Literally, "cast them down."
f "Baal of Peor": a Canaanite deity worshipped on Mt. Peor.

And the plague was checked;

³¹ And in all later generations that was seen as a sign of his righteousness.^{*a*}

³² They angered God^{*b*} at the waters of Meribah;^{*c*}

And it went badly for Moses because of them,

   ³³ For rash speech came from his lips^{*d*} when they rebelled against *God's* spirit.

³⁴ They did not destroy the *heathen* nations as the LORD commanded them.

Rather, they

   ³⁵ Mingled among the heathen and learned their customs;

   ³⁶ Served their idols, which became a snare to them; and

   ³⁷ Sacrificed their sons and their daughters to demons.

     ³⁸ They shed innocent blood,

       The blood of their sons and of their daughters,

       Whom they sacrificed to the idols of Canaan;

And the land was polluted with blood.

³⁹ They defiled themselves^{*e*} by their acts, and

They prostituted themselves by their deeds.

⁴⁰ Therefore the wrath of the LORD was kindled against his people,

   And he abhorred his own inheritance.

⁴¹ He gave them into the hand of the *heathen* nations,

   And those who hated them ruled over them.

   ⁴² Their enemies oppressed them,

   And they were brought into subjection under their power.

⁴³ Many times he delivered them,

But their plans were *only* rebellious—they sank in their sin.

⁴⁴ *Nevertheless,*

   He looked upon their distress when he heard their cry;

   ⁴⁵ For their sake he remembered his covenant;

   And, because of his unfailing love, he relented.

   ⁴⁶ He made them objects of compassion to all their captors.

⁴⁷ Save us, O LORD our God,

Gather us back from among the *heathen* nations,

   To give thanks to your holy name, and

   To glory in your praise.

Closing Doxology

⁴⁸ Blessed be the LORD God of Israel from everlasting to everlasting.

Let all the people say, "Amen."

Hallelujah!

---

a   Literally, "counted to him as righteousness."

b   Literally, "him."

c   Or "waters of strife," or "contention." A reference to Exodus 17:5-7

d   Literally, "he spoke rashly with his lips."

e   Literally, "they became unclean."

BOOK FIVE

Psalm 107
Give Thanks to the Lord

¹ Give thanks to the Lord;
 For he is good;
 For his lovingkindness endures forever.
² Let the redeemed of the LORD say,
 "He has redeemed us from the hand of the enemy;
 ³ He has gathered us out of the lands,
 From the east and from the west,
 From the north and from the south."

⁴ Some wandered in the desert wilderness, but could not find a way to a city to dwell in.
⁵ Hungry and thirsty, their soul fainted within them.
⁶ Then they cried to the LORD in their trouble,
And he delivered them out of their distress[a] ⁷ and he led them straight to a city to dwell in.

 ⁸ Let them give thanks to the LORD
 For his lovingkindness and
 For his wonderful works on behalf of the children of man,
 ⁹ For he satisfies the longing soul;
 And he fills the hungry soul with good things.

¹⁰ Some sat in darkness and in the shadow of death,
 Prisoners in misery and iron chains;
¹¹ Because
 They rebelled against the words of God and
 They spurned the counsel of the most High.
¹² Therefore
 He humbled their hearts with hard labor; and
 They fell down, and there was no one to help.
¹³ Then they cried to the Lord in their trouble,
 And he saved them from their distress.
 ¹⁴ He brought them out of darkness and the shadow of death, and
 He broke their bonds.

 ¹⁵ Let them give thanks to the LORD
 For his lovingkindness, and
 For his wonderful works on behalf of the children of man.
 ¹⁶ For he has broken down the brass prison gates, cut the iron bars.

---

a   Literally, "led them on a straight way to go to."

¹⁷ Fools suffered
> Because of their rebellious ways,
> Because of their sins.

¹⁸ They loathed every kind of food and came near the gates of death.

¹⁹ Then they cried to the Lord in their trouble,
And he saved them from their distress.
> ²⁰ He sent his word;
> He healed them;
> He delivered them from their destructions.

> > ²¹ Let them give thanks to the LORD
> > For his lovingkindness, and
> > For his wonderful works on behalf of the children of man.
> > ²² Let them offer the sacrifices of thanksgiving
> > And tell of his works with songs of joy.

²³ Those who go down to the sea in ships, who do business on the great waters

²⁴ see the works of the LORD and his wonders on the deep *seas*.
> ²⁵ For he speaks and the stormy wind rises up and lifts up the waves,
> > ²⁶ —*Waves* that rise up to the heavens and go down to the depths;
> > —Trouble that melts the soul.

²⁷ They reel *to and fro*, stagger like drunken men and *come to* their wit's end.

²⁸ Then they cry to the Lord in their trouble; and
He brings them out of their distress, ²⁹ makes the storm still, and hushes the waves.
> ³⁰ They are glad because it is quiet;
> And he guides them to their desired haven.

> > ³¹ Let them give thanks the LORD
> > For his lovingkindness, and
> > For his wonderful works on behalf of the children of man.
> > ³² Let them exalt him in the assembly of the the people
> > And praise him in the council of the elders.

³³ He turns
> Rivers into a wilderness;
> Springs of water into thirsty ground; and

³⁴ Fruitful land into salty wasteland,
> Because of the wickedness of those who dwell there;

³⁵ He turns
> The desert into pools of water, and
> Dry ground into springs of water.
> > ³⁶ There he lets the hungry
> > Dwell and establish a city to live in;
> > ³⁷ Sow the fields and plant vineyards; and

Gather a fruitful harvest.
38 By his blessing they multiply greatly;
He does not let their herds decrease.

39 When they are diminished, brought low by oppression, suffering and sorrow,
40 He pours contempt upon their leaders by making them wander in a trackless
wasteland;
41 He lifts the needy out of their affliction; and
Makes their families *increase* like flocks *of sheep.*
42 The righteous will see it and be glad,
And all the wicked will shut their mouths.

43 Whoever is wise,
Heed these things;
Consider the lovingkindness of the LORD.

Psalm 108
The Steadfast Heart

A song. A psalm of David.

1 O God,
My heart is steadfast;
I will sing praises with all my heart;
2 "Wake up, harp and lyre!"
I will awaken the dawn.
3 O LORD,
I will give thanks to you among the people;
I will sing your praises among the nations;
4 For your lovingkindness is higher than*ᵃ* the heavens,
And your faithfulness reaches to the skies.

5 O God,
Be exalted above the heavens;
May your glory *be exalted* above all the earth
6 That your beloved may be delivered.
Save us with your right hand and answer me.

7 God *once* spoke in his holiness*ᵇ* rejoicing:
"I will divide up Shechem and measure off the valley of Succoth;
8 Gilead and Manasseh are mine;
Ephraim is the helmet on my head;
Judah is my scepter;
9 Moab is my washpot;
I will throw my shoe*ᶜ* at Edom, and

---

a   Literally, "great above."
b   Or "from his sanctuary."
c   "Throw my shoe": an insulting gesture.

I will shout in triumph over Philistia."

¹⁰ *But now* who will bring me into the fortified city, lead me into Edom?
¹¹ God, haven't you rejected us?
God, you don't go out with our armies.
¹² Oh *God*, give us help against our enemies,
For deliverance by man is vanity.
¹³ With God we will act boldly,
For he will trample down our foes.

Psalm 109
Prayer Against the Wicked

A psalm of David.
To the music director.

¹ O God of my praise,
Do not be silent;
² For wicked and deceitful men have opened their mouths against me.
They
Speak against me with lying tongues;
³ Surround me with words of hatred;
Fight against me without a cause; and
⁴ Act against me in return for my love.
But I give myself to prayer.

⁵ They reward me with evil for good, hatred for love.
They say of me:
⁶ "Set a wicked man against[a] him, and
Let this accuser stand *to testify* at his right hand.
⁷ Let him be found guilty when he is tried, and
Let his prayers *for mercy* condemn him.
⁸ Let his days be few, and
Let another take his office.
⁹ Let his children be fatherless and his wife be a widow.
¹⁰ Let his children wander aimlessly[b] from their hovels, begging and seeking
food.
¹¹ Let his creditor seize all he has, and
Let the strangers plunder the fruit of his labor.
¹² Let no one extend lovingkindness to him, and
Let no one be gracious to his fatherless children.
¹³ Let his descendants die,[c] and
Let his name be blotted out in the next generation.

a Literally, "over."
b Literally, "wander wander" [sic].
c Literally, "be cut off."

¹⁴ Let the iniquity of his fathers be remembered before the LORD;
Let not the sin of his mother be blotted out.

But I say of them,
¹⁵ "Let their sin continually be before the LORD;
Let any memory of them be blotted out from the earth;
¹⁶ Because they
Did not remember to show lovingkindness, and
Persecuted the weak, needy and broken-hearted to the point of death.*ᵃ*
¹⁷ Since they loved cursing,
Let *curses*ᵇ come upon them;
Since they did not delight in blessing *others,*
Let blessings be far from them.
¹⁸ Since they clothed themselves with a garment of curses:
Let curses enter their bodies like water and their bones like oil;
¹⁹ Let them be the garment that covers them;
Let them be a belt continually strapped on *each of* them.
²⁰ Let this be yourᶜ reward for my accusers and for those who speak evil against my soul.
²¹ O LORD, my GOD,*ᵈ*
For the sake of your name, act on my behalf;
Out of your lovingkindness, deliver me.
²² For:
I am poor and needy, and
My heart is wounded within me.
²³ I am fading like the shadow at evening, and
I am shaking like a locust.
²⁴ My knees are weak from fasting, and
My body has grown lean and gaunt.
²⁵ I have become an *object* of scorn;
When they look at me they shake their heads.

²⁶ O LORD my God,
Help me;
Save me according to your lovingkindness,
²⁷ So they may know
That it is your hand;
That you, O LORD, have done it.
²⁸ Let them curse me, for I *know* you will bless me.
Let them be put to shame when they rise up,
And let your servant rejoice.

---

a Literally, "to put to death."
b Literally, "let it."
c Literally, "the LORD's."
d Or "O Sovereign LORD"

²⁹ Let my adversaries be clothed with dishonor;
Let their shame wrap them like a cloak.

³⁰ I will give abundant thanks to the LORD with my mouth;
I will praise him in the midst of the multitude;
   ³¹ For he stands at the right hand of the needy *person*
To save him from those who condemn his soul.

Psalm 110
David Sings of His Messiah

A psalm of David

 ¹ The LORD said to my Lord,
"Sit at my right hand until I make your enemies your footstool."
 ² The LORD will extend your strong scepter beyond Zion.
You will rule in the midst of your enemies;
  ³ Your people will volunteer *to serve* in the time of your power;
Like the dawn *provides* dew, *Israel's* wombs *will provide* youth *to serve.*^{*a*}
 ⁴ The LORD has sworn, and he will not change his mind,
"You are a priest forever in the order of Melchizedek."
 ⁵ The Lord is at your right hand.
He will:
Crush kings on the day of his wrath;
  ⁶ Judge the nations;
Fill *the lands* with the dead bodies;
Shatter the princes throughout the whole earth;^{*b*} and
 ⁷ Drink from the brook by the path.
Therefore he will be victorious.^{*c*}

Psalm 111
The Works of the Lord are Great

 ¹ Hallelujah!
I will give thanks to the LORD with all my heart,
In the assembly of the upright, in the congregation.
  ² The works of the LORD are great, studied by all who take pleasure in them;
  ³ His deeds are glorious and majestic;
His righteousness endures forever;
  ⁴ He made his wondrous works to be remembered.^{*d*}
The LORD is gracious and compassionate.

---

a Literally, "the womb of dawn the dew of youth." Verses three and four come from very cryptic Hebrew.
b Literally, "the broad country."
c Literally, "lift up his head."
d Or "has caused us to remember his wondrous works."

⁵ He gives food to those who fear him;
He always*ᵃ* remembers his covenant;
⁶ He has shown his people the power of his works;
He has given them the inheritance of *other* nations.

⁷ The works of his hands are faithful and just;
All his precepts are trustworthy.
⁸ They stand fast forever and ever,
And are to be performed in truth and uprightness.
⁹ He has sent redemption to his people;
He has ordained his covenant forever;
His name is holy and awesome.

¹⁰ The fear of the LORD is the beginning of wisdom;
All those who practice it have good understanding.
His praise endures forever.

Psalm 112
About the Righteous

¹ Hallelujah!

Blessed is the man
Who fears the LORD,
Who delights greatly in *obeying* his commandments.
² His descendants will be mighty upon the earth,
That generation of the upright will be blessed.
³ Wealth and riches are in his house, and
His righteousness endures forever.
⁴ His light shines in the darkness for the upright *to see.*
He is gracious and compassionate and righteous.

⁵ It goes well with people who
Deal generously,
Lend, and
Conduct their affairs with justice.
⁶ Surely they will never be shaken.

The righteous *person* will be remembered forever.
⁷ He will not be afraid of bad news.
His heart is fixed, trusting in the LORD;
⁸ His heart is steady until he looks triumphantly upon his enemies;
He is not afraid.
⁹ He has given freely to the poor;
His righteousness endures forever;
His horn will be exalted with honor.

---

a   Literally, "forever."

¹⁰ The wicked person will see this and be angry;
He will gnash his teeth and slink away.^a
The desire of the wicked will perish.

Psalm 113
Praise the Lord

¹ Hallelujah!
Praise him, O servants of the LORD;
Praise the name of the LORD;
² Blessed be the name of the LORD now and forever;
³ The LORD's name is to be praised from the rising of the sun to its setting;
⁴ The LORD is high above all nations;
His glory is above the heavens.

⁵ Who is like the Lord our God?
Who is seated on high?
⁶ Who stoops down to look upon heaven and the earth?
⁷ The Lord^b lifts the needy from the dust.
He lifts the poor out of the ash heap ⁸ to place them with princes,
Even with the princes of his people.
⁹ The barren woman abides in her house *and becomes* a joyful mother of children!
Hallelujah!

Psalm 114
The Lord Delivered Israel

¹ When Israel left Egypt,
When the house of Jacob *escaped* from that people with a strange language,
² Judah became God's sanctuary; Israel *became* his dominion.

³ The *Red* Sea saw this and fled!
The Jordan turned back *its flow!*
⁴ The mountains skipped like rams, and the little hills like lambs!
⁵ Why was it:
O sea, that you fled?
O Jordan, that you turned back?
⁶ You mountains, that you skipped like rams?
You hills, *that you skipped* like lambs?

⁷ Tremble, O earth,

---

a Literally, "melt," or "dissolve."
b Literally, "he lifts."

At the presence of the Lord,
At the presence of the God of Jacob
   8 Who turned the rock into a pool of water,
   Who turned the flint into a spring of water.

Psalm 115
Trust The Lord, Not Idols

1 Not to us, O LORD,
   Not to us—but to your name give glory
      Because of your lovingkindness and faithfulness.

2 Why do the nations ask, "Where is their God?"
   3 Because our God is in heaven, and
      He does whatever he pleases.
4 Their idols are silver and gold, the work of human hands.
   5 They have
      Mouths, but do not speak;
      Eyes, but do not see;
      6 Ears, but do not hear;
      Noses, but do not smell;
      7 Hands, but do not feel;
      Feet, but do not walk;
      Throats, but cannot make a sound.
   8 Those who make idols become like them, as do all those who trust in them.

9 Trust in the LORD, O Israel;
            He is your help and your shield.
10 Trust in the LORD, house of Aaron;
            He is your help and your shield.
11 You who fear the LORD, trust in the LORD;
            He is your help and your shield.

12 The LORD has remembered us.
      He will bless us;
      He will bless the house of Israel;
      He will bless the house of Aaron;
   13 He will bless those who fear the LORD, both small and great.

¹⁴ May the L<small>ORD</small> give you increase, both you and your children;^{*a*}
¹⁵ May you be blessed by the L<small>ORD</small> who made heaven and earth.
  ¹⁶ The heavens, *yes* the heavens, are the L<small>ORD</small>'s;
    But the earth he has given to the children of man.

¹⁷ The dead do not praise the L<small>ORD</small>,
    Nor do those who go down into silence;
¹⁸ But we will bless the L<small>ORD</small> now and forever.

Hallelujah!

Psalm 116
The Lord Is Gracious

¹ I love the L<small>ORD</small>,
    Because he has heard my voice and my prayers;
  ² Because he has inclined his ear to me.
      Therefore I will call upon him as long as I live.

³ The cords of death surrounded me;
  The pangs of Sheol^{*b*} gripped me; and
  I encountered trouble and sorrow.
⁴ Then I called upon the name of the L<small>ORD</small>, *crying out*
      "O L<small>ORD</small>, save my soul."

⁵ The L<small>ORD</small> is gracious and righteous;
  Our God is compassionate;
⁶ The L<small>ORD</small> protects the simple—I was brought low, and he saved me.
⁷ So return to your rest, O my soul,
    For the L<small>ORD</small> has been good to you;
  ⁸ For he has delivered
      My soul from death,
      My eyes from tears, and
      My feet from stumbling.
⁹ I will walk before the L<small>ORD</small> in the land of the living.
    (¹⁰ I believed *in you*
        Even when I said, "I am greatly afflicted,"
      ¹¹ *Even* when I was alarmed and said "All men are liars.")

¹² What will I give to the Lord in return for all his goodness^{*c*} toward me?
¹³ I will
    Lift up the cup of salvation;
    Call upon the name of the L<small>ORD</small>; and

---

a   Or "may the Lord add to your numbers, both yours and your children."
b   Or "of the grave."
c   Literally, "his benefits."

¹⁴ Pay my vows to the Lord in the presence of all his people.

¹⁵ Precious in the sight of the LORD is the death of his godly ones.
¹⁶ O LORD, truly
   I am your servant, *yes God*, your servant;
   I am the son of your maidservant; and
   You have freed me from my chains.
¹⁷ Therefore I will
   Offer to you the sacrifice of thanksgiving;
   Call upon the name of the LORD;
      ¹⁸ Pay my vows to the Lord
         In the presence of all his people,
            ¹⁹ In the courts of the LORD's house,
            In your midst, O Jerusalem.
   Hallelujah!

Psalm 117
Praise Him

¹ Praise the LORD, all you nations;
   Praise him, all you people;
      ² For his lovingkindness is so great toward us;
      And the faithfulness of the LORD endures forever.
   Hallelujah!

Psalm 118
Trusting in the Lord

¹ Give thanks to the Lord, for he is good;
               His lovingkindness endures forever.
² Let Israel say,
               His lovingkindness endures forever.
³ Let the house of Aaron say,
               His lovingkindness endures forever.
⁴ Let those who fear the LORD say,
               His lovingkindness endures forever.

⁵ I called upon the LORD in distress.
   The LORD answered me *and set me* free.*a*
⁶ The LORD is for me!
   I will not be afraid—what can man do to me?

---

a   Literally, "set me in a spacious place," or "answered me in a wide open place."

⁷ The Lord takes my side!
He is my help.
I will look in triumph over those who hate me.

⁸ It is better to take refuge in the Lord than to trust in man;
⁹ It is better to trust in the Lord than to trust in princes.
¹⁰ All *the hostile* nations surrounded me,
But in the name of the Lord I destroyed them.
¹¹ They surrounded me, completely surrounded me,
But in the name of the Lord I destroyed them;
¹² They surrounded me like bees,
But they were extinguished like the fire among thorns;
In the name of the Lord I destroyed them.
¹³ I was pushed back—falling,,
But the Lord helped me.
¹⁴ The Lord is my strength and song;
He has become my salvation.

¹⁵ Shouts of rejoicing and "Salvation" *resound* in the tents of the righteous:
"The right hand of the Lord has done mighty things.
¹⁶ Lift high *in triumph* the right hand of the Lord.
The right hand of the Lord has done mighty things."
¹⁷ So I will not die, but will live and declare the works of the Lord.
¹⁸ The Lord has chastened me severely,
But he hasn't given me over to death.
^{19a} Open the gates of righteousness to me,
²⁰ The gateways of the Lord through which the righteous enter.
^{19b} I will pass through them and give *thanks* to the Lord.
²¹ I will give thanks to you,
For you answered me;
And you have become my salvation.

²² The stone the builder rejected has become the cornerstone.
²³ The Lord did it!—it's marvelous for our eyes *to see.*
²⁴ This is the day the Lord has made—let us rejoice and be glad in it.

²⁵ Please Lord, save us;
Please Lord, please grant us success.

²⁶ Blessed is he who comes in the name of the Lord;
We bless you from the house of the Lord.
²⁷ The Lord is God and has made his light shine upon us,
So tie the festival sacrifice to the horns of the altar with cords.

²⁸ You are my God, and I will give you *thanks*;
You are my God, and I will exalt you.

²⁹ Give thanks to the Lord;
>> For he is good;
>> For his lovingkindness endures forever.

Psalm 119
Blessed Are the Undefiled

¹ Blessed are those whose way is blameless,
>> Who walk within the law of the LORD.
² Blessed are those who keep his statutes;
>> Who seek him with their whole heart;
>> ³ Who do no wrong;
>> Who walk in his ways.

⁴ You have commanded that your laws be kept diligently;
⁵ O that my ways were steadfast, *always* in line with^a your statutes;
>> ⁶ Then I would not be ashamed when I consider all your commands.

⁷ I will praise you with an upright heart as I learn your righteous rules;
⁸ I will keep your statutes;
Do not give up on me.^{b}

Keeping Your Way Clean

⁹ How can a young man keep his way pure?
>> By keeping it according to your word.
¹⁰ I am seeking you with my whole heart;
>> Do not let me wander from your commandments.
¹¹ I have hid your word in my heart
>> That I might not sin against you.
¹² Blessed are you, O LORD;
Teach me your statutes.

¹³ With my lips I have shared^c all the rules *spoken by* your mouth;
¹⁴ I have rejoiced living within the boundaries of your rules^d
>> As much as *others rejoice* in all *their* riches;
¹⁵ I meditate on your laws and observe your ways;
¹⁶ I delight myself in your statutes and will not forget your word.

¹⁷ Treat your servant with generosity,
>> That I may live and keep your word;
¹⁸ Open my eyes,
>> That I may see wondrous things in your law.

---

a Literally, "keeping."
b Literally, "utterly forsake me."
c Literally, "told of."
d Literally, "living the way of your laws."

¹⁹ I am a stranger*a* in this land;
Do not hide your commands from me.
²⁰ My soul is crushed, always longing for your laws.

²¹ You rebuke the arrogant,
Those cursed *people* who wander from your commands.
²² Remove reproach and contempt from me,
For I have kept your laws.
²³ Though princes sit and talk against me, your servant meditates on your statutes.
²⁴ The words you have spoken*b* are my delight, my counselors.

²⁵ My soul clings to the dust;
Revive me with your word.
²⁶ I have declared my ways and you have responded;
Now teach me your statutes;
²⁷ *Let me* understand the meaning*c* of your laws;
And I will meditate on your wondrous works.

²⁸ My soul weeps with sorrow.
Strengthen me with your word;
²⁹ Remove deceitful ways from me; and
Graciously give me *knowledge of* your law;
³⁰ For
I have chosen the way of truth.
I have set your judgments before me, and
³¹ I have held fast to your laws.
O Lᴏʀᴅ, don't let me be put to shame.
³² When you enlarge my heart, I will run in the path of your commandments.

Prayer for God's Law in My Life

³³ O Lᴏʀᴅ,
Teach me the way of your statutes,
And I will keep them until my end;
³⁴ Give me understanding,
And I will keep your law and follow it with my whole heart;
³⁵ Lead me in the path of your commandments,
For I delight in them;
³⁶ Turn my heart toward your laws and not to selfish gain;
³⁷ Turn my eyes away from looking at worthless things;
Restore me to your path;*d*

---

a Or "alien," or "sojourner."
b Literally, "your testimonies."
c Literally, "way."
d Or "revive me by your word."

³⁸ Establish your word in your servant,
>   That you may be feared;
³⁹ Take away my reproachful behavior,^{*a*} which I dread;
>   For your laws are good.

⁴⁰ O how I long for your laws;
> Give me a life^{*b*} of your righteousness.

O LORD,
⁴¹ Let your lovingkindness come to me;
>   Let your salvation *come to me* through your word;
>   ⁴² So I will have an answer for those who taunt me,
>   For I trust in your word.
⁴³ Do not take your word of truth completely from my mouth,
>   For I have placed my hope in your laws.
>   ⁴⁴ I will obey your law continually, forever and ever;
>   ⁴⁵ I will walk in freedom,^{*c*}
>   For I seek *to live by* your laws;
>   ⁴⁶ I will speak of your laws before kings and not be ashamed;
>   ⁴⁷ I will delight in your commands—how I love them!
>   ⁴⁸ I will lift up my hands to your commandments, love them and meditate on
>   your statutes.

God's Word Brings Hope

⁴⁹ Remember your word to your servant
>   In which you have made me hope.
⁵⁰ It is my comfort in my trouble;
> Your word revives me.
⁵¹ Though the arrogant mock me without restraint,^{*d*}
>   I have not turned away from your law;
>   ⁵² I remember your regulations of old, O LORD, and find comfort in them;
>   ⁵³ Burning *anger* has taken hold of me because the wicked forsake your law.
⁵⁴ In the houses of my pilgrimage,^{*e*} your statutes have been my songs.

⁵⁵ O LORD,
>   I remember your name in the night;
>   I keep your law;
>   ⁵⁶ This has become *my life:* keeping your laws.

---

a   Literally, "my reproach."
b   Or "revive me in your righteousness."
c   Literally, "a wide place."
d   Literally, "greatly."
e   Or "of my sojourning."

God is Our Portion

⁵⁷ You are my portion, O LORD.
    I have promised to keep your words;
    ⁵⁸ I have sought your favor with my whole heart—be gracious to me in
    accordance with your word;
    ⁵⁹ I have thought on my ways and turned my feet to *walk within* your laws;
    ⁶⁰ I hurry and do not delay to keep your commandments;
    ⁶¹ I do not forget your law even when the cords of the wicked encircle me;
    ⁶² I rise at midnight to give you thanks[a] for your righteous rules;
    ⁶³ I am a friend of all those who fear you and keep your laws.

⁶⁴ The earth, O LORD, is full of your lovingkindness,
  Teach me your statutes.

The Benefit of Affliction

⁶⁵ You have dealt well with your servant, O LORD,
    According to your word.
⁶⁶ Teach me good judgment and knowledge,
    For I believe in your commands.
    ⁶⁷ Before, when I was afflicted,[b] I went astray;
    But now I obey your word.
⁶⁸ You are good and do good;
  Teach me your statutes.

⁶⁹ The arrogant smear me with lies,
    But I will keep your laws with my whole heart;
⁷⁰ Their heart is covered with fat,[c]
    But I delight in your law.
⁷¹ It is good for me that I have been afflicted,
    That I might learn your statutes.
⁷² The law of your mouth is better to me than millions[d] in gold and silver.

Your Hands Fashioned Me

⁷³ Your hands made me and formed me;
    Give me understanding so I can learn your commandments.
⁷⁴ Let those who fear you rejoice when they see me,
    For I put my hope in your word;
    ⁷⁵ For I know, O LORD, that your laws are right;
    And *I know* that in *your* faithfulness you have afflicted me.

---

a Or "praise you."
b Or "before I was afflicted."
c "Covered with fat": a metaphor for unfeeling, callousness.
d Literally, "thousands." A thousand dollars in biblical days is more like a million today.

⁷⁶ May your lovingkindness be my comfort,
According to your promise*ᵃ* to your servant;
⁷⁷ Let your compassion come to me that I may live,
For your law is my delight.
⁷⁸ Let the arrogant be put to shame.
Though they wrong me with lies, I will continue meditating on your laws.
⁷⁹ Let those who fear you and know your laws turn to me.*ᵇ*
⁸⁰ Let my heart be blameless in *keeping* your statutes,
That I may not be put to shame.

Waiting for God's Help

⁸¹ My soul
Longs for your salvation, and
Waits in *the knowledge of* your word.
⁸² My eyes fail,
Searching for your promise,*ᶜ*
Asking,
"When will you comfort me?"
⁸³ Though I have become *shriveled* like a smoked wineskin, I have not forgotten your statutes.
⁸⁴ How many days *must* your servant *wait*?
When will you execute judgment on those who persecute me?
⁸⁵ The proud, who are not in accord with your law, have dug pits for me.

⁸⁶ All your commands are trustworthy.
Help me, for
They persecute me wrongfully;
⁸⁷ They have almost wiped*ᵈ* me off the earth,
But I *still* have not forsaken your laws.
⁸⁸ Let me live,
Because of your lovingkindness;
That I may continue to obey the things you command.*ᵉ*

God's Words Are Forever

⁸⁹ Forever, O Lᴏʀᴅ, your word is settled in heaven;
⁹⁰ Your faithfulness *extends* to all generations;
You established the earth, and it *still* stands;
⁹¹ Your laws *still* stand, *even to* today.
All things are your servants.

---

a Literally, "your word."
b Or "turn to me that they might know your laws," or "know your testimonies."
c Literally, "your word."
d Literally, "destroyed."
e Literally, "testimonies of your mouth."

⁹² If your law had not been my delight,
　　I would have perished in my affliction.
⁹³ I will never forget your precepts,
　　For you have given me life through them.

⁹⁴ I am yours;
　Save me,
　　For I have worked at obeying*a* your laws;
　　⁹⁵ I diligently consider your testimonies,
　　　But the wicked wait to destroy me.
　　⁹⁶ I see a limit to all *human* perfection,
　　　But your commands are without limit.*b*

The Law Brings Understanding

⁹⁷ O how I love your law;
　　　It is my meditation all day long.
⁹⁸ Your commands make me wiser than my enemies;
　　　Because they are always with me.
⁹⁹ I have more insight than all my teachers;
　　　Because what you have said is*c* my meditation.
¹⁰⁰ I understand more than my elders,
　　　Because I live by*d* your precepts.
¹⁰¹ I have restrained my feet from *walking in* any*e* evil way;
　　　So that I might keep your word;
¹⁰² I have not departed from your laws,
　　　For you *yourself* have taught me.
¹⁰³ How sweet are your words to my taste,
　　　Sweeter than honey to my mouth!
¹⁰⁴ Through your precepts I get understanding,
　　　Therefore I hate every false way.

Your Word Is a Lamp

¹⁰⁵ Your word is a lamp to my feet and a light to my path;
¹⁰⁶ I have sworn and confirmed an oath that I will keep your righteous rules.

¹⁰⁷ I am afflicted very much.
　　O Lᴏʀᴅ, revive me by your word;
　　¹⁰⁸ O Lᴏʀᴅ, accept the freewill offerings of my mouth;
　　O Lᴏʀᴅ, teach me your rules.
¹⁰⁹ Though my life is continually in my hand,*f*
　　I do not forget your law;

---

a　Or "understanding." Literally, "I have sought."
b　Literally, "are exceedingly broad."
c　Literally, "because your testimonies are."
d　Literally, "I keep."
e　Literally, "kept my feet from every."
f　"In my hand": a metaphor for at risk.

110 Though the wicked have set a snare for me,
    I do not stray from your laws;

111 Your laws are my heritage forever, the joy of my heart;
112 I have inclined my heart to perform your statutes forever, to the very end.

Single-Minded and Faithful

113 I hate double-mindedness;
    I love your law.
114 You are my hiding place and my shield;
    I hope in your word.
115 Depart from me, evildoers;
    I keep the commands of my God.

116 Sustain me according to your word,
    So I may live;
  Do not let me be ashamed of my hope *in you;*
117 Hold me up,
    That I may be safe,
    That I may continue to respect your statutes.

118 You have rejected all those who wander from your statutes,
    For their deceit is in vain;
119 You discard all the wicked of the earth like dross,*a*
    No wonder I love your testimonies;
    120 *No wonder* my flesh trembles in fear of you;
    No wonder I am afraid of your judgments.

Prayer of the Righteous

121 I practice justice and righteousness.
    Do not leave me to my oppressors;
    122 Pledge*b* good for your servant;
    Do not let the arrogant oppress me.
123 My eyes are exhausted looking for your salvation, the fulfillment of your word;

124 Deal with your servant according to your lovingkindness.
    Teach me your statutes;
    125 Give me understanding;
        For I am your servant;
        That I may understand what you have decreed.*c*
126 LORD, it's time for you to act—they are breaking your law.

127 I love your commandments more than gold, the purest gold;
128 I consider all your laws to be right; and

---

a   "Dross": the impure waste that floats to the top of molten metal.
b   Literally, "be surety for."
c   Literally, "your testimonies."

I hate every false path.

129 Your laws are wonderful,
> Therefore my soul obeys them;

130 The unfolding of your words gives light, gives understanding to the simple;

131 I open my mouth and pant, longing for your commands.

132 Turn to me;
Be gracious to me,
> *As is* your manner towards those who love your name;

133 Direct my steps by your word;
Let no sin rule over me;

134 Ransom me from the oppression of man,
> That I may keep your precepts;

135 Make your face shine upon your servant; and
Teach me your statutes.

136 Rivers of tears flow down from my eyes because people do not keep your law.

God Is Righteous

137 O LORD,
> You are righteous;
> Your laws are right;

138 You have decreed your laws in righteousness and great faithfulness;
> > (139 My zeal *for you* has consumed me, because my enemies have forgotten
> > your words.)

140 Your word is very pure;*ᵃ*
Your servant loves it.

141 I am lowly and despised,
> Yet I do not forget your laws;

142 Because your righteousness is an everlasting righteousness;
> And your law is truth.

143 Trouble and anguish have come upon me;
Yet your commandments are my delights.

144 The righteousness of what you say*ᵇ* is everlasting.
Give me understanding that I may live.

Crying Out to God

145 O LORD,
> I cry out with my whole heart.
> > Answer me—I will keep your statutes.

146 I cry out to you.
> > Save me—I will keep your laws.

147 I rise at dawn and cry out to you;

---

a   Or "is thoroughly tested."

b   Literally, "righteousness of your testimonies," or "your laws."

I hope in your word;
148 My eyes look forward to the nighttime,*a*
    So I can meditate on your word.
149 Hear my voice according to your lovingkindness, O LORD;
    Revive me according to your judgment.

150 Those who practice wickedness draw near.
    They live outside of*b* your law, but
151 You are near, O LORD, and all your commandments are true.
152 I have known for a long time that you founded your laws *to last* forever.

A Prayer for Deliverance

153 Look at my suffering and deliver me,
    For I have not forgotten your law;
154 Plead my case—redeem me;
    Revive me according to your word *to us.*
      (155 Salvation is far from the wicked,
        For they do not bother with*c* your statutes.)
156 O LORD, great are your mercies;
    Give me life in accordance with your laws.

157 My enemies and persecutors are many,
    But I have not turned from your testimonies;
158 I look at the treacherous with loathing;
    Because they do not keep your word.
159 Consider how I love your laws;
    Revive me, O LORD, as befits your lovingkindness.

160 The sum of your word is truth,
    And all your righteous rules will endure forever.

Standing With God in Persecution

161 Princes have persecuted me without a cause,
Yet
    My heart stands in awe of your word;
162 I rejoice at your word like one who finds great treasure;*d*
163 I hate and abhor falsehood;
    I love your law;
164 I praise you seven times a day for *giving us* your righteous rules.
    165 Those who love your law have great peace,
      Because nothing causes them to stumble.

---

a Literally, "night watches."
b Literally, "are far from."
c Literally, "don't seek."
d Literally, "great spoil."

¹⁶⁶ LORD,

I have hoped for your salvation;

I have followed your commandments;

¹⁶⁷ I^a have kept your testimonies—I love them exceedingly;

¹⁶⁸ I have followed your laws and your testimonies;

All my ways are before you.

A Cry for Understanding and Help

¹⁶⁹ O LORD,

Let my cry come before you:

"Give me understanding through your word."

¹⁷⁰ Let my plea come before you;

"Deliver me according to *the promise of* your word."

¹⁷¹ My lips will pour out praise,

For you have taught me your statutes;

¹⁷² My tongue will proclaim your word,

For all your commands are right.

¹⁷³ Let your hand help me,

For

I have chosen your precepts;

¹⁷⁴ I have longed for your salvation, O LORD; and

Your law is my delight.

¹⁷⁵ Let my soul live

And I will praise you,

And your laws will help me.

¹⁷⁶ I have strayed like a lost sheep;

Seek your servant,

For I have not forgotten your commands.

Psalm 120
A Cry for Deliverance from Deceivers

A song of ascents.

¹ In my distress I cried to the Lord;

He answered me *when I cried,*

² "Deliver my soul, O LORD,

From lying lips,

From a deceitful tongue."

³ O *you with* a false tongue,

What *punishment* will he give to you?

How will he *punish* you?

⁴ With sharp arrows from a mighty warrior!

With hot broom-wood coals!^b

---

a Or "my soul."

b "Broomwood coals": The coals of the broom plant, a desert shrub, burn especially hot.

⁵ Woe is me,

I'm tired of dwelling in Mesech and in the tents of Kedar.^{*a*}

⁶ I've dwelt with *these people* who hate peace for too long.

⁷ I'm for peace; but when I speak *of it*, they're for war.

Psalm 121
Our Help Comes from The Lord

A song of ascents.

¹ I will lift up my eyes to the hills.

Where does my help come from?

² My help comes from the LORD,

Who made heaven and earth.

³ He will not allow your foot to be moved;

He who watches over you will not slumber;

⁴ Behold, he who watches over Israel will neither slumber nor sleep.

⁵ The LORD is your keeper;

The LORD is your shade at your right hand;

⁶ The sun will not strike you by day, nor the moon by night.

⁷ The LORD will keep you from all evil;

He will preserve your soul.

⁸ The LORD will watch over you as you come and go,

Both now and forever.

Psalm 122
Jerusalem

A song of ascents of David

¹ I was glad when they said to me, "Let us go into the house of the LORD."

² *And now* our feet are standing within your gates, O Jerusalem.

³ Jerusalem was built

As a compact and united city

⁴ For the tribes (*i.e.,* the tribes of the LORD),

So they could go up to give thanks to the name of the LORD

According to the law *given to* Israel.

⁵ And the thrones of judgment, the thrones of the house of David, stand there.

⁶ Pray for peace in Jerusalem *like this,*

"May those who love you prosper.

⁷ Peace be within your walls;

Prosperity be within your palaces."

---

a "Mesech" and "Kedar," two peoples who did not follow God.

8 For the sake of my brothers and companions,
  I will pray, "Peace be within you."
9 For the sake of the house of the LORD our God,
  I will seek your good, *O Jerusalem.*

Psalm 123
A Prayer for Mercy

A song of ascents.

1 I lift up my eyes to you, you who are enthroned in the heavens.
2 Behold,
  As the eyes of servants *look* to the hand of their master, and
  As the eyes of a maidservant *look* to the hand of her mistress;
  So our eyes *look* to you, O LORD our God, until you have mercy on us.
3 Have mercy upon us, O LORD;
Have mercy upon us;
  For we are so filled to the brim*a* with *their* contempt;
  4 Our souls are fed up*b*
    With the ridicule of those who are at ease, and
    With the contempt of the arrogant.*c*

Psalm 124
Recognizing God's Deliverance

A song of ascents of David.

1 If The LORD Had Not Been On Our Side.

Leader:
  Now let Israel say:
Congregation:
  2 If the LORD had not been on our side when men rose up against us, 3 they
  would have swallowed us up alive when their wrath burned against us.
    4 That flood *of men* would have engulfed us;
    The torrent would have swept over us;
    5 Raging waters *of them* would have swept over our lives.
  6 Blessed be the LORD who has not given us *as prey* to be torn by teeth.
  7 We have escaped *just like* a bird *escapes* a fowler's snare.
    The snare is broken—we've escaped!
  8 Our help is from*d* the LORD, who made heaven and earth.

---

a Literally, "exceedingly full."
b Literally, "exceedingly full."
c Or "of the proud."
d Literally, "in the name of."

Psalm 125
The Lord Surrounds His People

A song of ascents.

¹ Those who trust in the Lord are like Mt. Zion,
  Which cannot be moved, but stays in place forever.
² Just as the mountains surround Jerusalem now and forever,
  The Lord surrounds his people.
³ The scepter of the wicked will not remain over the land of the righteous,
  Lest the righteous use their hands to do wrong.

⁴ O Lord, do good to those who are good, who are upright in their hearts.
⁵ Lord, lead away the evildoers, those who turn to crooked ways.[a]

Peace be upon Israel.

Psalm 126
Sowing in Tears, Reaping in Joy

A song of ascents.

¹ When the Lord brought back the captives to Zion,
  We were like those who dream.
    ² Our mouths were filled with laughter, our tongues with joyful song.
  Then it was said among the *heathen* nations,
    "The Lord has done great things for them."
³ The Lord has done great things for us,
  And we are glad.

⁴ Restore our fortunes, O Lord,
  As the streams of the south *renew the desert.*
⁵ Those who sow in tears will reap with shouts of joy.
    ⁶ He who goes out weeping and carrying seed to sow
  Will return with shouts[b] of joy, bringing his sheaves[c] with him.

Psalm 127
God Is Our Provider

A song of ascents of Solomon.

¹ Unless the Lord builds the house,
  They who build it labor in vain;

---

a   Or "the Lord will lead away those who turn to crooked ways."
b   Or "with songs."
c   "Sheaves": cut stalks of plants (typically wheat) bound together by straw or cord.

Unless the Lord watches over the city,
    The watchmen stay awake in vain.

2 It is vain to rise up early or stay up late toiling for food to eat;*a*
    For he gives his beloved sleep.*b*

3 Listen,
    Children are a heritage from the Lord;
    The fruit of the womb is a reward *from him.*
    4 The children of your youth are like arrows in a warrior's hands;
    5 Blessed is the man whose quiver is full of them;*c*
        When he speaks with the enemies at the *city* gates, he will not be put to shame.

Psalm 128
Blessed Is Everyone Who Fears The Lord

A song of ascents.
  1 Blessed are all
    Who fear the Lord,
    Who walk in his ways.
      2 You will eat the fruit *of the labor* of your hands;
      You will be blessed;
      It will be well with you;
      3 Your wife will be like a fruitful vine in your home;
      Your children around your table will be like *young* olive trees.
  4 Yes, indeed,
  The man who fears the Lord will be blessed.

5 May the Lord bless you from Zion;
  May you see Jerusalem prosper*d* all the days of your life.
6 May you see your children's children.
  Peace be upon Israel.

Psalm 129
Against the Wicked

A song of ascents.

1 Many times they have persecuted*e* me since my youth.
  May Israel now declare:

---

a Literally, "to eat the bread of painful *labor.*"
b Or "for he gives to his beloved as he sleeps."
c Or "the man who fills his quiver with them."
d Literally, "see the prosperity of Jerusalem."
e Or "afflicted."

2 "Many times have they persecuted*a* me since my youth,
But they have not prevailed against me
Even though
3 The plowmen plowed upon my back;*b*
They lengthened their furrows *on me.*
4 The Lord, being righteous, has cut the ropes of the wicked."

5 May all who hate Zion be put to shame and turned back;
6 May they be like grass upon the housetops
Which withers before it grows up;
7 Which cannot fill a reaper's hands or a sheaf-binder's*c* arms.*d*
8 May no one who passes by say *to them*:
"The blessing of the Lord be upon you," *or*
"We bless you in the name of the Lord."

Psalm 130
Waiting Upon the Lord

A song of ascents.

1 Out of the depths I cry to you, O Lord.
2 Lord, hear my voice;
Let your ears be attentive to the voice of my supplications.
3 If you, Lord, recorded our sins—O Lord, who could stand?
4 But with you there is forgiveness,
That you might be feared.

5 I wait for the Lord.
My soul waits, and
I hope in his word.
6 My soul *waits* for the Lord
More than the watchman in the morning,
Yes, more than the watchman in the morning.

7 Israel, hope in the Lord;
For with the Lord there is lovingkindness;
And with him there is full*e* redemption;
8 He will redeem Israel from all its sins.

a Or "afflicted."
b "Plowed upon my back": a metaphor for being cut upon the back.
c "Sheaf-binder": one who gathers and binds the cut stalks of wheat or similar plants.
d Literally, "sheaf-binder's bosom" (a picture of his arms holding stalks against his breast).
e Or "there is plenty of."

Psalm 131
Content Before the Lord

A song of ascents of David

¹ Lord,

> My heart is not proud;
> My eyes are not haughty;
> I do not involve myself with great matters, *things* beyond me.^{*a*}

² I have calmed and quieted my soul,

> Like a child weaned from its mother;
> My soul within me is like a weaned child.

³ Likewise, let Israel wait for the Lord, now and forever.

Psalm 132
David's Devotion and God's Promise

A song of ascents.

¹ Lord, in support of David, remember all his struggles^{*b*} *for you;*

> ² How he swore *an oath* to you, O Lord;
> How he made a vow to you, the Mighty One of Jacob, *saying:*
>> ³ "I will not
>>> Enter the shelter^{*c*} of my house;
>>>> ⁴ Lie on my bed; or
>>>> Give sleep to my eyes or slumber to my eyelids
>>> ⁵ Until I find
>>>> A place for you, O LORD,^{*d*}
>>>> A dwelling place for the Mighty One of Jacob."^{*e*}
> ⁶ Remember,
>> It was we who heard about *the Ark of the Covenant being* at Ephratah;
>> And we who recovered it^{*f*} in the fields of Jaar.

⁷ Let us go into the sanctuary of the LORD;^{*g*}

Let us worship at the footstool *of his throne, saying:*

> ⁸ "O LORD,
>> Rise up;
>> *Come* into your resting *place,* you and the ark of your might;

---

a Literally, "great matters, too..."

b Or "his hardships."

c Literally, "the tent."

d David is referring to finding a place to build a permanent temple (to replace the travelling tabernacle) in which the Ark of the Covenant (over which God's presence was constantly manifested) will be placed.

e David is referring to his vow to build a permanent temple as God's dwelling place.

f Literally, "we found it."

g Literally, "into his dwelling place."

⁹ Let your priests be clothed with righteousness;
Let your godly ones sing for joy;
¹⁰ Do not turn away from the face of your anointed;
For the sake of your servant, David."

¹¹ The LORD swore an oath to David,
A sure oath he will not turn from:
"I will place one of your descendants^a upon your throne.
¹² If your sons obey my covenant and the rules that I teach them,
Then their sons will also sit upon your throne forever.

The Lord & Jerusalem

¹³ The LORD has chosen Zion;
He has desired it for his dwelling place.
He has said:
¹⁴ "This is my resting place forever and ever;
I will dwell here because I want to.
¹⁵ I will bless her with abundant provisions;
I will satisfy her poor with bread."
¹⁶ I will clothe her priests with salvation,
And her godly ones will shout for joy.

---

¹⁷ "I will increase David's strength.^b
I have prepared a lamp for my anointed *one*.
¹⁸ I will clothe his enemies with shame,
But on him his crown will shine."

Psalm 133
Family Unity

A song of ascents of David.

¹ Look,
How good and pleasant it is for brothers to dwell together in unity.
² It is
Like good oil *poured* on a head that runs down onto a beard
Such as Aaron's beard, flowing down to the edge of his robe;
³ Like the dew of *Mt.* Hermon; and
Like the dew that descends upon the mountains of Zion;
For there the LORD pronounced his blessing—life everlasting.

---

a   Literally, "the fruit of your body."
b   Literally, "make the horn of David sprout."

Psalm 134
Bless and Be Blessed

A song of ascents of David.

¹ Come, all you servants of the LORD who serve in the house of the LORD at night.
Bless the LORD:
   ² Lift up your hands in the sanctuary;
   Bless the LORD.

³ May the LORD who made heaven and earth bless you from Zion.

Psalm 135
Praise the Lord

¹ Hallelujah!
Praise the name of the LORD;
Praise him
   You servants of the LORD;
   ² You who stand
      In the house of the LORD;
      In the courts of the house of our God.
³ Praise the LORD,
   For the LORD is good.
Sing praises to his name,
For
   It is pleasant;
   ⁴ The LORD has chosen Jacob for himself,
      Israel as his treasured possession.

⁵ I know that the LORD is great, and
Our Lord is above all gods.
   ⁶ The LORD does all that he pleases
      In the heavens and on earth,
      In the seas and all the deep *places*.
   ⁷ He makes the clouds ascend from the ends of the earth;
   He makes the lightning and the rain;
   He brings the wind out of his storehouses.

   ⁸ He struck down the firstborn of Egypt,
      Both man and beast;
   ⁹ He sent signs and wonders into the midst of Egypt,
      Against Pharaoh and all his servants;

¹⁰ He struck down many nations and killed mighty kings:
  ¹¹ Sihon, king of the Amorites;
  Og, king of Bashan; and
  All the kings of Canaan;
¹² He gave their land as an estate,
  An estate for his people, Israel.
    (¹³ Your name, O L ORD, endures forever;
      Your renown, O L ORD, *endures* through all generations.)
¹⁴ The L ORD judges *on behalf of*[a] his people,
  And he has compassion on his servants.

¹⁵ The idols of the *heathen* nations are *made of* silver and gold;
They are the work of men's hands.
  ¹⁶ They have mouths, but do not speak;
  They have eyes, but do not see;
  ¹⁷ They have ears, but do not hear;
  Nor is there breath in their mouths.
¹⁸ Those who make them will be like them;
And so will everyone who trusts in them.

¹⁹ House of Israel, bless the L ORD;
House of Aaron, bless the L ORD;
²⁰ House of Levi, bless the L ORD;
You who fear the L ORD, bless the L ORD;
²¹ Blessed is the L ORD from Zion, he who dwells at Jerusalem.
Hallelujah!

Psalm 136
His Lovingkindness Endures Forever

  ¹ Give thanks to the Lord, for he is good;
          His lovingkindness endures forever;
  ² Give thanks to the God of gods;
          His lovingkindness endures forever;
  ³ Give thanks to the Lord of lords;
          His lovingkindness endures forever.
  Give thanks to him
    ⁴ Who alone performs great wonders;
          His lovingkindness endures forever;
    ⁵ Who with wisdom made the heavens;
          His lovingkindness endures forever;
    ⁶ Who stretched out the earth upon the waters;
          His lovingkindness endures forever;

---
a   Or "The L ORD will vindicate."

⁷ Who made great lights;
>> His lovingkindness endures forever;
>> ⁸ The sun to rule over the day;
>> His lovingkindness endures forever;
>> ⁹ The moon and stars to rule over night;
>> His lovingkindness endures forever.
¹⁰ Who struck down the firstborn of Egypt;
>> His lovingkindness endures forever;

¹¹ Who brought Israel out from their midst;
>> His lovingkindness endures forever;
>> ¹² With a mighty hand and an outstretched arm;
>> His lovingkindness endures forever;
¹³ Who split apart the Red Sea;
>> His lovingkindness endures forever;
¹⁴ Who made Israel pass through the midst of it;
>> His lovingkindness endures forever;
¹⁵ Who hurled Pharaoh and his army into the Red Sea;
>> His lovingkindness endures forever;
¹⁶ Who led his people in the wilderness;
>> His lovingkindness endures forever;
¹⁷ Who struck down great kings;
>> His lovingkindness endures forever;
¹⁸ Who killed mighty kings;
>> His lovingkindness endures forever;
>> ¹⁹ Sihon, king of the Amorites;
>> His lovingkindness endures forever;
>> ²⁰ And Og, king of Bashan;
>> His lovingkindness endures forever;
²¹ Who gave their land as an estate;
>> His lovingkindness endures forever;
>> ²² As an inheritance to his servant Israel;
>> His lovingkindness endures forever;

²³ Who remembered us when we were low;
>> His lovingkindness endures forever;
²⁴ Who delivered us from our enemies;
>> His lovingkindness endures forever;
²⁵ Who gives food to all flesh;
>> His lovingkindness endures forever.

²⁶ Give thanks to the God of heaven;
>> His lovingkindness endures forever.

Psalm 137
Remembering Jerusalem in Babylon

¹ By the streams of Babylon
    We sat and wept when we remembered Zion;
    ² We hung our harps upon the poplars.
    ³ Our captors tormented us, asking us to sing joyful songs,
        Saying, "Sing one of the songs of Zion!"
    ⁴ But how can we sing the LORD's song on foreign soil?

⁵ If I forget you, O Jerusalem,
    Let my right hand wither.*^a*
⁶ If I do not remember you,
  If I do not prefer Jerusalem above my highest joy,
    Let my tongue cleave to the roof of my mouth.

⁷ Remember, O LORD, the sons of Edom in the day of Jerusalem's *fall*,
    When they said, "Destroy it; tear it down to its foundation."
⁸ O daughter of Babylon, *doomed to be* destroyed,*^b*
    Blessed be*^c* whoever repays you, repays you as you have dealt with us;
    ⁹ Blessed be*^d* whoever seizes your little ones and hurls them against the rocks!

Psalm 138
Praising God With a Whole Heart

A psalm of David.

¹ I give you thanks with my whole heart;
  I will sing praise to you in front of their *imaginary* gods;
² I bow down toward your holy temple;
  I praise your name for your lovingkindness and your faithfulness;
  For
    You have exalted your word and your name above all things.
    ³ On the day I called, you answered me and strengthened my soul.
⁴ All the kings of the earth will praise you, O LORD,
    When they hear the words of your mouth.
⁵ They will sing of the ways of the LORD;
    For great is the glory of the LORD.

⁶ Though the LORD is *on* high, he sees the lowly;
    But he keeps his distance from*^e* the proud.
⁷ Though I walk in the midst of trouble,

---

a   Or "let my right hand forget."
b   Literally, "O daughter of devastated Babylon."
c   Or "blessed will be," or "happy is."
d   Or "blessed will be," or "happy is."
e   Literally, "knows from afar."

You will give me life despite my enemies' wrath;
You will stretch out your hand;
Your right hand will save me.

[8] The LORD will accomplish what *he wants* for me.[a]
O LORD, your lovingkindness endures forever.
Do not abandon *me*, the work of your own hands.

Psalm 139
The Ever-Present All-Knowing God

A psalm of David.
To the music director.

[1] O Lord,
You have searched me, and you know me.
> [2] You know when I sit down and when I get up;
> You understand my thoughts from afar;
> [3] You search out my path and my place of rest;[b]
> You are familiar with all my ways.
> [4] There is not a word on my tongue—behold, O LORD, you know it all.
[5] You have hemmed me in, *both* in front and back;
You have laid your hand upon me.
[6] Such knowledge is so wonderful—so high I cannot grasp[c] it.

[7] Where can I go *to escape* from your spirit?
Where can I flee from your presence?
> [8] If I soar to the heavens, you are there;
> If I bed down in Sheol—behold, you are there *too!*
> [9] If I take *flight on* the wings of the morning,
> If I dwell in the ends of the sea,
> > [10] Even there your hand will lead me,
> > And your right hand will take hold of me;
> [11] Surely, if I ask the darkness to cover me and the light around me to
> become night—[12]even the darkness is not dark to you!
> > To you the night is as bright as the day—darkness is like light!

[13] You created my innermost parts;
You wove me in my mother's womb.
[14] Thank you that I am fearfully and wonderfully made.
> Your works are marvelous and my soul knows it very well;
> [15] My frame[d] was not hidden from you when I was made in secret, skillfully
> woven[e] in the depths of the earth;

---

a   Literally, "the Lord will fulfill for me."
b   Literally, "of lying down."
c   Literally, "cannot attain."
d   Or "my strength," or "my bones."
e   Or "intricately woven."

¹⁶ Your eyes saw my unformed substance;
Everything was written down in your book—*all* the days that were
ordained for me;
Though not one of them had *yet* come to be.^{*a*}
¹⁷ How precious also are your thoughts *about me*, O God;
How great is the sum of them.
¹⁸ If I count them, they would be more than the sand.
And when I wake up, you are still with me!^{*b*}

¹⁹ Surely you will slay the wicked, O God,
(Depart from me therefore, you bloody men.)
²⁰ For they scheme against you;
And your enemies take your name in vain.^{*c*}

²¹ O LORD,
How I hate those who hate you;
How I detest those who rise up against you;
²² I hate them—hate them totally!
They have become my enemies.

²³ Search me, O God, and know my heart;
Examine me and know my thoughts.
²⁴ See if there is any wicked way^{*d*} in me; and
Lead me in the path of everlasting *life*.

Psalm 140
Deliver Me from the Evil Man

A psalm of David.
To the music director.

¹ Deliver me, O LORD, from evil people;
Preserve me from violent men
² Who plan evil things in their heart;
Who stir up battles every day;
³ Who sharpen their tongues like a serpent;
Who have viper's poison on their lips.   Selah
⁴ Keep me, O LORD, from the hands of the wicked;
Preserve me from violent men who plan to trip my feet.

⁵ The proud have hidden a trap for me;
With cords they have spread a net on my path;
They have set snares for me.   Selah

---

a   Or "and not one of them lacked." The Hebrew is not clear.
b   Literally, "I am still with you."
c   Or "your enemies falsely swear," or "your enemies misuse your name."
d   Literally, "vexing way" (i.e., something that annoys or bothers God).

⁶ *So* I said to the Lord,
  "You are my God.
  Hear the voice of my pleas, O Lᴏʀᴅ.
  ⁷ O Lᴏʀᴅ, my God, the strength of my deliverance,
    You have protected*ᵃ* my head in the day of battle.
    ⁸ Do not grant the desires of the wicked, O Lᴏʀᴅ;
    Do not let their wicked plans advance, or they will be exalted.*ᵇ*   Selah
    ⁹ Let the mischief of their own lips overwhelm*ᶜ* those who surround me;
    ¹⁰ Let burning coals rain upon them;
    Let them be cast into the fire, into deep pits*ᵈ* from which they cannot rise.
    ¹¹ Let no slanderer*ᵉ* be established on the earth.
    Let calamity*ᶠ* hunt down the violent man."

¹² I know that the Lᴏʀᴅ will maintain
  The cause of the afflicted and
  Justice for the poor.
¹³ Surely the righteous will praise*ᵍ* your name;
  The upright will dwell in your presence.

Psalm 141
Lord, Keep Me from Evil

A psalm of David.

¹ Lord,
  I cry out to you, "Come quickly."
  Turn your ear to my voice when I cry out to you.
  ² Let
    My prayer stand before you as incense, and
    My uplifted hands be my evening sacrifice.
  ³ Guard my mouth, O Lᴏʀᴅ;
    Set a guard at the door of my lips.
  ⁴ Do not incline my heart to anything evil:
    To wicked acts with evil doers;
    Don't *even* let me eat their delicacies.
      ⁵ *If I do,*
        Let the righteous smite me;
          It will be a kindness.
        Let them reprove*ʰ* me;
          It will be a *healing* oil—my head will not refuse it.

---

a   Literally, "have covered."
b   Or "will become proud."
c   Literally, "cover the heads of."
d   Or "into ravines."
e   Literally, "man of the tongue."
f   Literally, "evil."
g   Or "give thanks to."
h   "Reprove": express disapproval.

For I pray continually against their wicked deeds.

6 When *evil* leaders are thrown off the cliff, they will remember[a] my words, for they were pleasant. Then *they will mourn:*

7 "Our bones are scattered at the mouth of Sheol like plowed and broken earth."[b]

8 My eyes are toward you, O Sovereign LORD;[c]

In you I take refuge.

Do not leave me exposed;

9 Keep me from the snares laid for me, the traps of evildoers;

10 Let the wicked fall into their own nets while I pass by *safely.*

Psalm 142
You Are My Refuge

A maskil of David.
A prayer when he was *hiding* in the cave.[d]

1 I cry to the Lord with my voice;

I plead before the Lord with my voice;

2 I pour out my complaint before him;

I tell him my trouble 3 when my spirit faints within me.

Lord,

You know my path;

They have laid a trap for me in the path I walk.

4 Look to the right and see:

No one has regard for me;

I have no refuge;

No one cares about my soul.

5 So I cry out to you, O Lord, praying,

"You are my refuge.

You are my portion in the land of the living."

6 Listen to my cry,

For I have been brought very low;

Deliver me from my persecutors,

For they are too strong for me;

7 Bring me out of this prison

That I may praise your name.

The righteous will gather around me,

For you will treat me generously.

---

a Literally, "hear."

b The Hebrew of verses six and seven is not clear.

c Or "O GOD, my Lord."

d A reference to I Samuel 22 or 24.

Psalm 143
A Prayer for the Troubled

A psalm of David.

¹ O L<small>ORD</small>,

> Hear my prayer;
> Turn your ear to my supplications;
> Answer me
>> In your faithfulness and
>> In your righteousness.

² Do not come to a verdict^{*a*} about your servant,

> For in your sight no one living is righteous.
>> ³ In my case, my enemy has
>>> Persecuted^{*b*} me;
>>> Driven^{*c*} me to the ground; and
>>> Made me live in darkness like a long dead person.

> ⁴ My spirit within has fainted;
> My heart within is stunned.
>> ⁵ I remember the days of old, *when*:
>>> I meditated^{*d*} on all your deeds;
>>> I spoke of^{*e*} the work of your hands;
>>>> ⁶ I thirsted like a parched land—stretched out my hands to you.   *Selah*

⁷ O L<small>ORD</small>,

> Quickly, hear me;
>> For my spirit is at its end;
> Do not hide your face from me,
>> So I won't be like those who have gone down to the pit;

⁸ Let me hear your lovingkindness in the morning,

> For I trust in you;

Let me know the way in which I should walk,

> For I lift up my soul to you;

⁹ Deliver me from my enemies, O L<small>ORD</small>,

> For I have fled to you for refuge;^{*f*}

¹⁰ Teach me to do your will,

> For you are my God;

Let your good spirit lead me to level ground.

---

a   Or "judgment."
b   Or "pursued."
c   Literally, "crushed."
d   Or "I spoke of."
e   Or "I meditated on."
f   Literally, "cover."

¹¹ O Lᴏʀᴅ,
>> Preserve me
>>> For your name's sake;
>> Bring my soul out of trouble
>>> For your righteousness' sake;
> ¹² Cut off my enemies
>> Out of your lovingkindness;
> Destroy all those who afflict my soul;
>> For I am your servant.

Psalm 144
Blessed Lord, Delivers Us

A psalm of David.

¹ Blessed be the Lᴏʀᴅ;
>> My rock who trains my hands for war and my fingers for battle;
> ² My loving God;
> My fortress;
> My stronghold;
> My deliverer;
> My shield;
> He in whom I take refuge;
> He who subdues people under me.

³ Lᴏʀᴅ,
>> What is man that you should know him,
>> Or mankind*^a* that you should think about him?
> ⁴ Man is but a breath;
>> His days are but a passing shadow.

⁵ Lᴏʀᴅ,
>> Part the heavens and come down;
>> Touch the mountains so they smoke;
> ⁶ Flash lightning and scatter your enemies;
>> Shoot out your arrows and panic them;
> ⁷ Stretch out your hand from on high;
>> Rescue me and deliver me out of the mighty *overwhelming* waters,
>>> Out of the foreigner's hand
>>>> ⁸ Whose mouth speaks falsely,
>>>> Whose right hand is a hand of lies.*^b*

---

a   Literally, "the son of man."

b   "Hand of lies": Perhaps a reference to raising the hand and swearing falsely.

⁹ I will sing a new song to you, O God;
Upon a ten stringed harp will I sing praises to you
¹⁰ Who gives victory to kings,
Who delivers his servant David from the evil sword.
¹¹ Deliver me and rescue me from the hand of the foreigner;
Whose mouth speaks falsely, and
Whose right hand is a right hand of lies.*ᵃ*
¹² Let our sons in their youth be like full grown plants;
Let our daughters be like corner-pillars carved for a palace;
¹³ Let our barns be full, hold*ᵇ* every kind *of crop*;
Let our flocks produce thousands, *even* ten thousands in our fields;
¹⁴ Let our oxen bear heavy loads;*ᶜ*
Let there be no breach of our walls, no loss and screaming in our streets.

¹⁵ Happy are the people who are thus *blessed.*
Happy are the people whose God is the Lord.

Psalm 145
God Is Great and Near

A psalm of praise of David.

¹ I will exalt you, my God and king;
I will bless your name forever and ever;
² Every day will I bless you, and
I will praise your name forever and ever *like this:*
³ "Great is the Lord, and worthy*ᵈ* to be praised;
His greatness is unfathomable."*ᵉ*

⁴ One generation will praise your works to the next generation;
They will tell about your mighty acts, and
⁵ I will meditate on the glorious splendor of your majesty and on your wondrous works.
⁶ They will speak about the power of your awesome deeds, and
I will proclaim your greatness.
⁷ They will eagerly speak about their memory of your great goodness,
And they will sing joyfully about your righteousness,

---

a "Hand of lies": Perhaps a reference to raising the hand and swearing falsely.
b Literally, "provide."
c Or "Let our oxen bear heavy young."
d Literally, "highly."
e Or "is unsearchable."

Singing:

> ⁸"The LORD is
>> Gracious,
>> Full of compassion,
>> Slow to anger, and
>> Full of lovingkindness.
>> ⁹ The LORD is good to all,
>> And his tender mercies are over *all* his works."

¹⁰ All your works will praise you, O LORD;
Your godly ones will bless you.
¹¹ They will speak of the glory of your kingdom
And talk of your power ¹² so mankind*^a* will know
> Your mighty acts,
> The glory of your reign,*^b*
>> ¹³ Your kingdom is an everlasting kingdom, and that
>> Your dominion *endures* throughout all generations.
¹⁴ *You* LORD,*^c*
> Hold up all who are falling,
> Are faithful in your words and kind in your works,*^d* and
> Straighten up all those who are bent over.
¹⁵ The eyes of all *mankind* look to you
> Who gives them food in due season,
>> ¹⁶ Who opens his hand and satisfies the desire of every living thing.

¹⁷ The LORD is righteous in all his ways and kind in all his works;
¹⁸ The LORD is near to all those who call upon him,
> To all who call upon him in truth.
¹⁹ He fulfills the desires of those who fear him;
> He hears their cry and rescues them.
²⁰ The LORD preserves all those who love him,
But he destroys all the wicked.

²¹ My mouth will speak in praise of the LORD.
Let all mankind*^e* bless his holy name forever and ever.

---

a   Literally, "to the sons of men."

b   Or "kingdom."

c   Though in Hebrew this verse is a statement about the Lord ("The LORD holds up all who are..."), due to the context, we present it as part of the psalmist's words to the Lord.

d   This verse has weak manuscript evidence, but is in the Septuagint.

e   Literally, "all flesh."

Psalm 146
Trust in God, Not Princes

¹ Hallelujah!
Praise the LORD, O my soul.
² As long as I live will I praise the LORD;
I will sing praises to my God as long as I live.

³ Do not trust in princes—in *mere* sons of men in whom there is no *lasting* help.[a]
⁴ Their breath[b] departs;
They return to dust;[c]
And on that day their thoughts cease.
⁵ Everyone who has the God of Jacob for his help is blessed·
Their hope is in the LORD, their God.
⁶ Who made heaven and earth, the sea and all that is in it;
Who is faithful[d] forever;
⁷ Who executes justice for the oppressed; and
Who gives food to the hungry.

The LORD sets the prisoners free;
⁸ The LORD gives sight to[e] the blind;
The LORD raises those who are bent over;[f]
The LORD loves the righteous;
⁹ The LORD protects the foreigners *among us*;
He sustains the fatherless and the widow;
And he thwarts the way of the wicked.

¹⁰ The LORD will reign forever;
He is your God, O Zion, for all generations.
Hallelujah!

Psalm 147
God Does It All

¹ Hallelujah!
It is good to sing praises to our God;
It is sweet to adorn him with praise[g] *like this:*

² "The LORD is building up Jerusalem;
He is gathering together the scattered of Israel.

---

a   Or "no salvation." Literally, "no deliverance."
b   Or "their spirit."
c   Literally, "the ground."
d   Literally, "keeps faith."
e   Literally, "opens the eyes of."
f   Or "bowed down."
g   Or "it is pleasant and fitting to praise him."

³ He heals the brokenhearted and bandages^a their wounds.

⁴ He determines the number of stars and calls them by name.

⁵ "Great is our Lord, abounding in power;
His understanding is infinite.
⁶ The LORD sustains^b the humble,
And he casts the wicked to the ground."

⁷ Sing to the Lord with thanksgiving;
Sing praise with the harp to our God who
⁸ Covers the heavens with clouds;
Readies rain for the earth;
Makes the grass spring up on the mountains;
⁹ Gives the beast his food; and
Feeds the young crying ravens.
¹⁰ He is not pleased by the might of a horse;
He takes no pleasure in the thighs of a man;
¹¹ *Rather,* the LORD delights in those who fear him, who put their hope in his lovingkindness.

¹² Praise the LORD, O Jerusalem;
Praise your God, O Zion;
¹³ For
He strengthens the bars of your gates;
He blesses your children within you;^c
¹⁴ He makes peace within your borders;
He satisfies *your hunger* with choice wheat.
¹⁵ He sends down his commandments to earth—O how quickly his word spreads!^d
¹⁶ He gives snow like wool;
He scatters the frost like ashes;
¹⁷ He hurls down hail as fragments—who can endure in his cold?
¹⁸ Then he sends out his word and melts them;
The wind blows; *they thaw;* and the waters flow.
¹⁹ He speaks his word to Jacob, his statutes and laws to Israel.
²⁰ He has not dealt this way with any *other* nation—they don't *even* know his laws!
Hallelujah!

---

a   Literally, "binds."
b   Or "the Lord encourages."
c   Or "children within your midst."
d   Literally, "his word runs."

Psalm 148
Everyone, Praise The Lord

¹ Hallelujah!
   Praise the LORD from the heavens;
   Praise him on the heights;
² Praise him, all his angels;
   Praise him, all his heavenly hosts;
³ Praise him, sun and moon;
   Praise him, all you shining stars;
⁴ Praise him, highest heavens and you waters above the heavens.

⁵ Let them praise the name of the LORD,
   For
        He commanded, and they were created;
        ⁶ He established them forever and ever;
        He gave a decree, and it will not pass away.

⁷ Praise the LORD from the earth,
        You sea monsters in all the ocean depths;ᵃ
        ⁸ Fire and hail, snow and clouds;ᵇ
        Stormy wind that performs his command;
        ⁹ Mountains and all the hills;
        Fruit trees and all cedars;
        ¹⁰ Wild beasts and all cattle;
        Crawling things and winged birds;
        ¹¹ Kings of the earth, all people, princes and all rulers of the earth;
        ¹² Young men and maidens;
        Old men and children.

¹³ Let them praise the name of the LORD,
   For
        His name alone is exalted;
        His glory is above the earth and heaven;
        ¹⁴ He has raised up the strengthᶜ of his people, Israel, a people close to him,
              For the gloryᵈ of all his godly ones.
   Hallelujah!

---

a   Or "monsters and all the deep."
b   Or "snow and smoke."
c   Literally, "the horn."
d   Or "the praise."

Psalm 149
Sing and Fight

¹ Hallelujah!
  Sing to the Lord a new song;
  Sing his praise in the assembly of his godly ones.
    ² Let Israel rejoice in its Maker;
      Let the children of Zion rejoice in their King;
    ³ Let them praise his name in dance;
      Let them sing praises with the tambourine and the harp.
⁴ For the LORD takes pleasure in his people;
  He will adorn the lowly with salvation.
⁵ Let his godly ones be joyful in this glory;
    Let them sing joyfully upon their couches;^a
      ⁶ Let the high praises of God be in their throats;
      Let a two-edged sword be in their hand
        ⁷ To wreak vengeance upon the *heathen* nations
            And punishments upon the people;
        ⁸ To bind their kings with chains
            And their nobles with shackles of iron;
        ⁹ To carry out the written judgment.
      Let this be the glory of all his godly ones.
  Hallelujah!

Psalm 150
Praise Him

¹ Hallelujah!
    Praise God in his sanctuary;
    Praise him throughout his universe;^b
    ² Praise him for his mighty acts;
    Praise him according to his abundant^c greatness;
    ³ Praise him with the sound of the ram's horn;
    Praise him with the harp and lyre;
    ⁴ Praise him with tambourines and dancing;
    Praise him with stringed instruments and flutes;
    ⁵ Praise him with the loud cymbals;
    Praise him with the crashing cymbals;
      ⁶ Let everything that has breath praise the LORD.
  Hallelujah!

---

a Or "their beds."
b Or "his heavens." Literally, "his mighty expanse."
c Literally, "great greatness."

Psalms Glossary[a]

The Readable Bible uses the same words that we use in everyday conversation as much as possible. Words that are not used in secular life are defined in footnotes if they are only used once or twice, and in the Glossary if they are used more often. The Glossary also includes geographic terms and words that we may use in our conversation, but which have specific meanings in the Psalms that differ from our usage.

Acclaim	To praise a person publicly and enthusiastically by shouting and cheering.
According to	On the basis of, and in line with the principle or qualities of. Appropriate.
Amen	So be it. An expression of affirmation, total agreement.
Anoint	To pour or smear oil (often, olive oil, sometimes perfumed) on a person as a symbol of the presence or power of God. Anointing is often done as part of a ceremony setting a person apart for a specific purpose and/or to install them in a position or office (e.g., priest).
Bashan, Mt. Bashan	A fertile area east and northeast of the Sea of Galilee, including the Golan Heights.
Benjamin	A tribe of Israel.
Bless, blessed	God towards man: to watch over, protect, bestow holiness upon. (e.g., "God will bless us.") Man towards God: to declare approval and support. To praise, glorify. (e.g., "I will bless the Lord.") Man towards man: to call upon God for his care of someone. (e.g., "May God bless you.")
Children of man/men	A metaphor for mankind.
Covenant	A solemn agreement.
Cush	The region south of Egypt (today divided among Eritrea, Sudan and Ethiopia).
Dismayed	Filled with alarm and distressed. Completely discouraged or disappointed.
Distress	Mental suffering caused by grief, anxiety and/or unhappiness.
Ephraim	One of the largest tribes in Israel, sometimes used as a metaphor for the whole nation.
Establish	To make firm or settle in a secure position. Regarding man's work, it suggests success.
Exalt	To glorify, honor or praise. To elevate in rank or status.
Exult	To be very happy, triumphant.
Face shine upon	Look on with favor and/or love.
Fear	Regard with reverent respect and awe.

a   This list of terms defines them as they are used in the Book of Psalms.

Fool	Someone who does not perceive, or does not recognize God' claim on his life.
Fruit	The produce of a person's labor, or the edible food of a plant.
Glory	Verb: To exalt, praise and give honor with emotion (as fans do when their favorite team wins a championship). Noun: The manifestation of God's presence and his character that man sees in his creation and his acts, and in his presence when he shows himself visibly.
GOD	When "YAHWEH" appears after "adonai" (A Hebrew term of reverence for God), we render the two words as "Lord GOD."
Godly ones	Those who trust in God, who obey his commands and look to him for strength and deliverance. The faithful.
Hallelujah!	Two words, "hallelu" and "jah." "Hallelu," the second person imperative, is a call for joyful praise. "Jah" is a short form of "Yahweh," the name of God. Therefore, "Praise God." Because of the emotion that pours out with "halle," we always follow hallelujah with an exclamation point.
Ham, land of	Egypt. Noah's son, Ham, is the ancestor of the Egyptians and other North East African peoples (Gen. 10:6ff)
Harp	The Israelites had three types of stringed instruments: harps, lyres and lutes. The Hebrew words for these stringed instruments do not signify which is meant. "Harp" is rendered when only one instrument is mentioned, and "lyre" when a second instrument is mentioned.
Heathen	The unconverted. Those who do not acknowledge God as their god, and thus live without regard for him.
Higgaion	Its meaning is uncertain. Perhaps a musical notation.
Hope	To have a sure confidence, firm expectation..
Hosts	Many people massed together, often for battle. Heaven's armies.
Inheritance (God's)	Israel. This expression indicates his relationship with Israel: they are his possession (by adoption), to be done with as he pleases.
Iniquity	Great injustice, extreme immorality.
Jacob	Isaac's son. His name is often used as a metaphor for Israel.
Jeduthun	The name of a Levitical singer and music leader at the time of King David. Some believe the word may also be a liturgical term, or may refer to a tune or a stringed instrument.
Judah	A tribe of Israel named after the fourth son of Jacob. The name is often used as a metaphor for Israel.
Justice	See "Righteousness."

LORD	The name of God is four Hebrew letters represented in English by YHWH (pronounced "YAHWEH"). Out of reverence for God's name, we render the word as "LORD" wherever his name appears except when the context calls for his actual name (in which case we supply the vowels and render his name as "YAHWEH.") The Hebrew may be translated "He who is," "He who exists," "He who causes to exist", or "He who gives life." French Bible translations render YHWH as "l'Eternel" (i.e., "The Eternal").
Lovingkindness	Our primary translation of the Hebrew word, "chesed." This word expresses a part of God's character which cannot be fully expressed by any English word. It includes loyal love, steadfast love, faithful love, kindness and mercy. We use "lovingkindness" unless another of these terms seems to best fit in light of the surrounding text, but please consider all these qualities each time you read "lovingkindness."
Lowly	Our primary translation of the Hebrew term "anah." This term is often translated as "humble" or "afflicted," and sometimes as "poor." Unless the context signifies one of those meanings, we use the term "lowly" to encompass all three meanings.
Lyre	See "Harp."
Magnify	Increase the apparent size or importance of a person.
Manasseh	A tribe of Israel. The older of the two sons of Joseph and Asenath.
Maskil	The term's meaning is unclear. Some believe it is a psalm used for teaching wisdom or piety; others, a poem for meditation.
Mt. Zion	Originally, a high point upon which Zion (today's Jerusalem) was built. A metaphor for Jerusalem, which is sometimes a metaphor for Israel.
Miktam	The term's meaning is unclear. Some believe it means "golden psalm." Others, a psalm of atonement.
Music director	Our translation of the Hebrew term "natsach." It might mean "choir director," or simply "leader."
Oil	Usually from olives. Used as a healing, soothing substance.
Ox	A castrated bull of domesticated cattle, used primarily for pulling a plow or cart.
Parable	A story with a moral lesson.
Poor	Not necessarily without wealth, but lacking the physical or spiritual resources necessary for the situation.
Princes	A general term for leaders, rulers and/or nobles.

Rahab	The Hebrew name Rahab translates as "proud one," but it is sometimes used as a metaphor for Egypt. In Job "Rahab" refers to a sea monster symbolizing forces contrary to God's order.
Rebuke	Noun: a strong criticism. Verb: To criticize sharply.
Reproach	Noun: a cause of disgrace or shame. Verb: to bring into discredit, or to point out someone as a cause of disgrace or shame.
Right hand	A metaphor for God's power.
Righteousness	Our primary translation of the Hebrew word "tsedeq." It is the state of being innocent before God. It also has a sense of justice (of treating others as the law stipulates), and treating others fairly.
Sackcloth	Crude coarse clothes worn to show mourning on account of sin, the loss of a loved one or other tragedy.
Salem	A short form of Jerusalem. See Zion.
Salvation	Peace with God. Deliverance in battle or from evil people.
Sanctuary	Where God dwells. Sometimes a reference to God's home in Heaven, sometimes to the Holy of Holies, that part of the Temple where God manifested himself above the Ark of the Covenant.
Scepter	A rod held in the hand of a royal person. Originally used as a weapon, it became a symbol of power.
Selah	The meaning of this Hebrew term is uncertain. It is generally believed to be a musical notation (e.g., interlude, repeat). Since its meaning is unclear and it adds nothing meaningful to Scripture, we present it in light text at the right side margin.
Sheol	The place of the dead who are not with God. Sometimes it refers to a person's grave.
Sinner	A person who openly disobeys God's laws.
Song of ascents	"Ascents" is a translation of the Hebrew term, "ma'alah"; which refers to things that go up in height or degree. "Song of ascents" may be a reference to the way the psalm is to be sung; or, it may mean it is to be sung as worshipers ascend up the paths to Jerusalem to celebrate the feasts.
Sons of men	A metaphor for mankind.
Steadfast love	See "lovingkindness."
Supplication	An earnest and sincere request.
Transgression	An act that violates a law (especially, God's law), command or moral code.
Trust	Firm reliance on and confidence in the integrity, ability, or character of a person.

Vain, vanity	Lacking substance or worth. Fruitless, useless. Deceitful. Sometimes this refers to idols.
Vindicate	Show that a person is without blame.
Wicked, the	Those who ignore God's reign, law and salvation; who openly sin against God.
Wilderness	An area destitute of vegetation. Used in the Readable Bible when the land has desert characteristics but is not sandy.
YAHWEH	See LORD
Zoan	An ancient city of the Nile delta (aka: Tanis).
Zion	A metaphor for Jerusalem, which is sometimes a metaphor for Israel. Originally a city on Mt. Zion captured by David. Jerusalem was built upon and around it.

Psalms by Subject

Comfort	23.
Confidence in God	3, 4, 11, 16, 23, 27, 29, 33, 46, 47, 56, 57, 58, 62, 63, 64, 66, 85, 89, 91, 108, 110, 121, 125, 131, 140
Creation	8, 19
Celebrations of Zion	46, 48, 76, 84, 87, 122
Cries, Complaints and Pleas for Help	4-7, 10, 12, 13, 17, 22, 25, 26, 28, 31, 35, 38, 39, 41, 43, 44, 53-57, 59, 60-64, 69-71, 74, 77, 79, 80, 82-4, 86, 88-90, 94, 102, 106, 109, 120, 123, 126, 129, 130, 137, 139-143
Gratitude	9, 18, 30, 32, 34, 40, 65, 66, 67, 107, 116, 118, 124, 136, 138
Historical. Records of God's Involvement With Israel	78, 105, 106, 135, 136
Kingship of God	47, 93, 96, 97, 98, 99
Mercy	32, 51, 130, 143
Praise for God as Protector and Benefactor of Israel	66, 100, 111, 114, 149
Praise for God as Creator	8, 19, 104, 148
Praise for God as the Lord of History	33, 103, 105, 106, 135, 145, 147
Praise, Other	24, 29, 45, 47, 93, 96, 97, 98, 99, 100, 117, 134, 144, 146, 150
Prayer for Another Person	20, 72
Prayer for Protection	34, 52, 54, 56, 59, 61, 140, 141, 142, 143
Salvation History. Records of God's actions on behalf of Israel.	78, 105, 106, 135, 136
Sovereignty of God	95, 96, 97, 98, 139
Thanksgiving	8, 18, 21, 30, 32, 34, 40, 65-67, 92, 107, 108, 113, 116, 118, 124, 136, 138,
Truths for Meditation	2, 8, 9, 10-12, 14, 15, 19, 23, 24, 26, 34, 36, 39, 42, 49, 50, 53, 73, 76, 77, 82, 89, 90, 94, 95, 97, 101, 103, 104, 115, 125, 132, 138, 139, 141, 144, 145
Victory, Celebration	18, 68
Wisdom. Psalms that present truths of God and/or praise Godly living.	1, 36, 37, 49, 52, 73, 75, 81, 82, 95, 112, 115, 119, 127, 128, 133, 139

Familiar Verses in Psalms

1:1-3	[1] Blessed is the man who does not walk in the counsel of the wicked, stand in the way of sinners, or sit in a seat with scoffers. [2] But his delight is in the law of the LORD, and in his law he meditates day and night. [3] He is like a tree planted by streams of water that yields its fruit in season, and whose leaf does not wither. Whatever he does prospers.
8:1	O LORD, our LORD, how majestic is your name throughout all the earth.
8:4	What is man, that you remember him?
12:6	The words of the LORD are pure words; like silver refined in a furnace, purified seven times.
14:1	The fool says in his heart, "There is no God."
16:5	LORD, you are my portion, my inheritance and my cup. You uphold my lot *in life*."
18:2	The LORD is my rock, my fortress, my deliverer, my God, my rock in whom I take refuge, my shield, the horn of my salvation, and my safe place.
18:28	You light my lamp.
18:30	As for God, his way is perfect.
18:46	The LORD lives. Blessed be my Rock. Exalted be the God of my salvation.
19:1	The heavens declare the glory of God.
19:7-10	[7] The law of the LORD is perfect, reviving the soul. The testimony of the LORD is perfect, making wise the simple. [8] The precepts of the LORD are right, bringing joy to the heart. The commands of the LORD are pure, enlightening the eyes. [9] The fear of the LORD is pure, enduring forever; The judgments of the LORD are true and righteous altogether; [10] To be desired more than gold, yes, *more than* lots of pure gold; sweeter than honey dripping off the honeycomb.
19:14	O LORD, my strength and my redeemer, let the words of my mouth and the meditation of my heart be acceptable in your sight.
20:7	Some trust in chariots, some *trust* in horses, but we trust in the name of the LORD our God.
22:1	My God, my God, why have you forsaken me?
22:9	You are the one who brought me out of the womb.
22:14	I am poured out like water. All my bones are out of joint.
22:18	They divide my garments among themselves. They cast lots for my clothes.

23:1-4	[1] The LORD is my shepherd; I shall not want. [2] He makes me lie down in green pastures. He leads me beside still waters. [3] He restores my soul. He leads me in the paths of righteousness for his name's sake. [4] Even though I walk through the valley of the shadow of death, I will fear no evil.
23:6	Surely goodness and lovingkindness will pursue me all the days of my life, and I will dwell in the house of the LORD forever.
24:3-4	[3] Who will ascend the mount of the LORD? Who will stand in his holy place? [4] He who has clean hands and a pure heart. He who does not lift up his soul to vanity or swear deceitfully.
24:8	Who is this King of glory? The LORD—strong and mighty. The LORD—mighty in battle.
27:4	One thing I ask of the Lord; *one thing* I seek: that I may dwell in the house of the LORD all the days of my life.
32:7	You are my hiding place.
34:7	The angel of the LORD encamps around those who fear him, and delivers them.
39:4	*Help me* know my end, the number of my days, how many they are; that I may know how fleeting my life *really* is.
40:1	I waited patiently for the LORD, and he bent down to me and heard my cry.
40:17	I am poor and needy, yet the Lord thinks of me!
42:1-2	[1] As the deer yearns for streams of water, so my soul yearns for you, O God. [2] My soul thirsts for God, the living God.
46:1	God is our refuge and strength, an ever-present help in *times of* trouble.
47:1	Clap your hands, all you people. Shout to God with cries of joy.
48:1	Great is the LORD, and to be praised greatly in the city of our God, on his holy mountain.
51:2-3	[2] Wash me thoroughly from my iniquity. Cleanse me from my sin. [3] For I know my transgressions, and my sin is always before me.
51:7	Purge me with hyssop, and I will be clean. Wash me, and I will be whiter than snow.
51:10	Create in me a clean heart, O God; and renew a right spirit within me.
51:17	The sacrifices of God are a broken spirit, a broken and repentant heart.
53:1	The fool says in his heart, "There is no God." Also, 56:22.
57:7	My heart is steadfast, O God. My heart is steadfast.
62:1	My soul waits in silence for God alone. My salvation comes from him.
63:3	Because your lovingkindness is better than life, my lips will praise you.
68:19	Blessed be the Lord who bears our burdens every day.
69:9	Zeal for your house consumes me.

84:1	How lovely is your dwelling place, O LORD of hosts.
84:10-11	¹⁰ For a day in your courts is better than a thousand *anywhere else.* I would rather be a doorkeeper in the house of my God than dwell in the tents of the wicked. ¹¹ For the LORD God is a sun and shield. The LORD gives grace and glory. He withholds no good thing from those who walk uprightly.
85:10	Righteousness and peace have kissed each other.
86:5	For you, Lord, are good; ready to forgive and abounding in lovingkindness to all who call upon you.
86:11	Teach me your ways that I may walk in your truth. Unite my heart to fear your name.
86:15	But you, O Lord, are a God who is merciful, gracious, slow to anger, and abounding in lovingkindness and truth.
90:4	To you a thousand years in your sight are like yesterday when it has passed, like a watch in the night.
90:12	Teach us to number our days.
91:1	He who dwells in the shelter of the Most High will abide in the shadow of the Almighty.
92:1	It is good to give thanks to the LORD.
92:5	O LORD, how great are your works. How very deep are your thoughts.
93:1	The LORD Reigns. Also, 97:1, 99:1.
94:9	He who implanted the ear, doesn't he hear?
94:12	Blessed is the man you discipline.
94:22	The LORD is my fortress.
95:1	Come, let us sing to the LORD. Let us shout to the rock of our salvation.
96:1	Sing a new song to the LORD. Sing to the LORD, all the earth.
97:5-6	⁵ The hills melt like wax before the LORD, before the Lord of the whole earth. ⁶ The heavens proclaim his righteousness. All people see his glory.
100:3-4	³ Know that the LORD himself is God. He made us—we're his, his people, the sheep of his pasture. ⁴ Enter into his gates with thanksgiving, into his courts with praise.
100:5	The LORD is good. His mercy endures forever; and his faithfulness continues through all generations.
103:1-2	¹ Bless the LORD, O my soul, and all that is within me, bless his holy name. ² Bless the LORD, O my soul, and do not forget all his benefits.
103:3-5	³ Who forgives all your sins. Who heals all your diseases. ⁴ Who redeems your life from the pit. Who crowns you with lovingkindness and compassion. ⁵ Who satisfies your years with good things so that your youth is renewed like a *soaring* eagle.

178

103:14-17	14 For he knows what we are made of, remembers that we are dust. 15 As for man, his days are like grass; he flourishes like a flower in a field. 16 When the wind passes over it, it is no more; and the place *where it was* no longer knows *that it ever was.* 17 But the lovingkindness of the Lord is over those who fear him from everlasting to everlasting.
104:5	You set the earth on its foundation so it will never totter.
105:5	Seek the Lord. Seek his strength. Seek his face continually.
107:1	Give thanks to the Lord; for he is good. For his lovingkindness endures forever.
111:10	The fear of the Lord is the beginning of wisdom.
112:5	It goes well with people who deal generously, lend and conduct their affairs with justice.
115:4-5	4 Their idols are silver and gold, the work of human hands. 5 They have mouths, but don't speak; eyes, but don't see.
115:8	Those who make idols become like them, as do all those who trust in them.
118:1	Give thanks to the Lord, for he is good; his lovingkindness endures forever.
118:8-9	8 It is better to take refuge in the Lord than to trust in man. 9 It is better to trust in the Lord than trust in princes.
118:22	The stone the builder rejected has become the cornerstone.
118:24	This is the day which the Lord has made—let us rejoice and be glad in it.
118:26	Blessed is he who comes in the name of the Lord.
119:9	How can a young man keep his way pure? By keeping it according to your word.
119:73	Your hands made me and formed me.
119:89-91	89 Forever, O Lord, your word is settled in heaven. 90 Your faithfulness extends to all generations. You established the earth, and it still stands. 91 Your laws still stand, even to today. All things are your servants.
119:105	Your word is a lamp to my feet and a light to my path.
119:136	Rivers of tears flow down from my eyes because people do not keep your law.
121:1-2	1 I will lift up my eyes to the hills. Where does my help come from? 2 My help comes from the Lord, who made heaven and earth.
122:1	I was glad when they said to me, "Let us go into the house of the Lord."
126:5	Those who sow in tears will reap with shouts of joy.
127:1	Unless the Lord builds the house, they who build it labor in vain; Unless the Lord watches over the city, the watchmen stay awake in vain.

127:3-4	3 Children are a heritage from the LORD. The fruit of the womb is a reward *from him.* 4 The children of your youth are like arrows in a warrior's hands. Blessed is the man whose quiver is full of them.
128:1	Blessed are all who fear the LORD, who walk in his ways.
135:15-16	15 The idols of the *heathen* nations are *made of* silver and gold. They are the work of men's hands. 16 They have mouths, but do not speak. They have eyes, but do not see.
136:1ff	His lovingkindness endures forever. *Repeated twenty-six times.*
139:1-2	1 O Lord, You have searched me, and you know me. 2 You know when I sit down and when I get up.
139:7-8	7 Where can I go to escape from your spirit? 8 Where can I flee from your presence?
139:12	To you the night is as bright as the day—darkness is like light!
139:13-16	13 You created my innermost parts. You wove me in my mother's womb. 14 Thank you that I am fearfully and wonderfully made. Your works are marvelous and my soul knows it very well. 15 My frame was not hidden from you when I was made in secret, skillfully woven in the depths of the earth. 16 Your eyes saw my unformed substance. Everything was written down in your book—*all* the days that were ordained for me; though not one of them had *yet* come to be.
144:3-4	3 What is man that you should know him, or mankind that you should think about him? 4 Man is but a breath. His days are but a passing shadow.
145:3	Great is the LORD, and worthy to be praised.
145:7	The LORD is gracious, full of compassion, slow to anger and full of lovingkindness
146:3-4	3 Do not trust in princes—in *mere* sons of men in whom there is no *lasting* help. 4 Their breath departs. They return to dust, and on that day their thoughts cease.
147:10-11	10 He is not pleased by the might of a horse. He takes no pleasure in the thighs of a man. 11 Rather, the LORD delights in those who fear him, who put their hope in his lovingkindness.
150:6	Let everything that has breath praise the LORD.

180

Key Persons in Psalms in order of appearance

Person	Key Facts	Psalms Where Mentioned. Bold face if only in inscription.
David[a]	The second king of Israel. He led Israel in its period of greatest expansion and power.	**3-9**; *11-32*; *18:50*, **34-41**; **51-65**; **68-70**; *72:20*; *77:20*; *78:70, 72*; **86**; *89:3, 20, 29, 35, 49*; **101**; **103**; **108-110**; *122:5*; **124**, **131**, *132:1, 10; 11, 17*; **133-134**, **138-143**, **144**:*10* **145**
Absalom	Son of David who led a revolt against him.	3
Cush, the Benjamite	An unknown person. The Benjamites fought with Saul against David.	**7**
Saul	A Benjamite, the first king of Israel.	**18**, **52**, **54**, **57**, **59**, 62:3
Jacob	Grandson of Abraham, son of Isaac. Patriarch of Israel.	**22:23**; **77:15**; **78:5, 21**; **105:10**; **105:23**
Abimelech	King of Gerar.	**34**
Sons of Korah (Korahites)	Descendants of the grandson of Kohath, a son of Levi. They were Temple singers who also did other work in the Temple.	**42**, **44-49**, **84-85**, **87-88**
Asaph	A descendant of Kohath, a son of Levi, who led the Temple music during the reigns of David and Solomon.	**50**, **73-83**
Solomon	David's son who was king of Israel during its time of greatest wealth. Known for his wisdom.	**72**, **127**
Joseph	Son of Jacob. Led Egypt during the years of plenty and famine; and gave shelter there to his father and brothers.	*77:15*; *78:67*; *80:1*; *81:5*; *105:17*
Aaron	Brother of Moses who assisted Moses, and who led the golden calf revolt against him.	*77:20*
Moses	Led Israel out of Egypt and in the forty years of wandering.	77:20, 90, 99:6; 103:7; 105:26, 106:16, 23, 32;
Heman, the Ezrahite	A Levite song leader during David's reign.	**88**
Ethan, the Ezrahite	Brother of Heman who played instruments.	**89**
Abraham	Patriarch who is the father of the Jews, of Israel.	105:6, 9, 42;

[a] Many inscriptions have "David" in the superscription preceded by the Hebrew particle "le." This is rendered as "of David." Traditionally this has been viewed as meaning the psalm was written by David, but it may mean that the psalm is for him, or is written in the style of David.

Translation Principles[a]

The Readable Bible is a literal translation in the sense that each original language word is expressed in English. However, sometimes a literal translation makes it probable that the reader will not understand the thought of the writer. For instance, people unfamiliar with ancient culture probably do not understand the command to "kiss the king." It is a command to show him homage, to make a formal public acknowledgement of allegiance. So, when the literal translation might confuse or mislead today's reader, a thought for thought translation is presented and the literal translation is footnoted, or vice versa.

As is common in modern translations, the words are not always expressed in the grammatical form of the original because occasionally that creates awkward English sentences. So we choose the grammatical form and sentence construction that we believe the writer would have chosen if he were a native English speaker.

Many Hebrew words have several meanings. While we render the meaning that we believe fits the context best, if an equally viable alternate term or phrase would give the text a significantly different sense or feel, we provide it in a notation.

Sometimes a psalmist left out words that he knew the singers and listeners would have in their minds due to their familiarity with the context, culture and language. Today, three thousand years later, English speaking readers need these words added to the text. Thus, we supply them in italics. Occasionally, for clarity or ease of reading, we substitute a noun for a pronoun, or vice versa.

Italicized additions to the text are used to clarify the text or avoid confusion for readers who (a) are not familiar with Scripture truths and the history of Israel, and (b) might not recognize when figures of speech (e.g., hyperbole, metaphors) are being used. For instance, Psalm 40:6 reads "You did not desire sacrifice and offering." The Readable Bible inserts "only" before "sacrifice and offering" to make the reading reflect the true meaning of the statement.

We have not capitalized personal pronouns that refer to God (as there is no such distinction in the original manuscripts) unless capitalizing clarifies the sentence.

Format and Presentation Notes

Our goal is to present you with a text that you can read with ease so that each psalm will flow off your tongue as it would have flowed off the tongue of a 21st century native English speaker.

Hebrew psalms are structured as poems. They are full of metaphor and have a rhythm of thought that is often quite complex. If you read Hebrew and are familiar with Hebrew poetry, you will sense their structure. A native English speaker reading English quickly senses the structure of a limerick or the musical feel of iambic meter (e.g. "I think that I shall never see...."). However, English readers do not sense the Hebrew poetry when reading it in English. Therefore, the Readable Bible formats the Psalms as cascading text. This style will (a) help you find the meaning of the text, (b) help you to see how phrases relate to each other, and (c) help you discover the rhythm of parallel phrases and thoughts.

---

[a] In the sections about translation, formatting and presentation principles I use the term "we" to honor the valuable input of many people who have provided constructive criticism and other input.

Cascading text shows how each thought of each verse relates to the previous and following thoughts. Reinforcing and subsidiary thoughts are indented. This helps the reader pick out the primary thoughts and see how they are supported by the secondary and tertiary thoughts. You will also notice parallel structures and parallel wording, and your understanding will increase.

We provide a topical heading for each psalm. These, placed under the psalm number, are not part of the inspired text. The text of some psalms starts with an inscription (e.g., "A Psalm of David"). These are numbered as the first verse in the Hebrew Bible, but are not numbered in Chrisitan Bibles. The inscriptions give us information such as the name of the author, when the psalm was written, the tune to which it is sung, or for whom it was written.

Seven Psalms (14, 45, 53, 55, 71, 99, and 32) have interludes in them. These are set off by lines. After you read the interlude, go back to the verses before it and read directly down to the verses under it to re-connect to the Pslamist's flow of thought.

We have not capitalized personal pronouns that refer to God (as there is no such distinction in the original manuscripts) unless capitalizing clarifies the sentence.

In some instances it is not possible to make a certain translation because of our imperfect understanding of ancient Hebrew and/or the apparent disorder of the Hebrew text. Such instances are annotated as "unclear." Some ancient Hebrew words are unknown today. When a word's meaning is uncertain, we provide a footnote about its meaning, or a translation and a footnote with the transliteration and/or alternate translations.

The word "literally" appears more often than any other word in The Readable Bible annotations. This is because we use the term to reveal occasions where we have moved from the literal (i.e., simplest, most direct) translation of a word and rendered another translation. This may be because we have rendered a thought-for-thought translation when the literal translation has a high probability of misleading the average reader. The "To The Reader" section at the front of the book gives an example of this from Psalm 16:7

We also add a "literally" footnote when we substitute a single word or two for a longer phrase. For instance, in the second sentence of Exodus 33:7 we substitute "go there" for "go out to the Meeting Tent which was outside the camp" (as the first sentence, which "there" refers to, has the same location information). And we provide a "literally" footnote when we combine expressions into one because the second one implies the first. For instance, in Exodus 33:8 the text says "the people got up and stood." Since a person cannot stand without getting up, The Readable Bible simply reads, "the people stood," and we footnote the literal translation.

Notes

Notes

Proof

22609163R00106

Made in the USA
Charleston, SC
24 September 2013